Careers in Focus

Writing

Ferguson Publishing Company
Chicago, Illinois

Careers in focus. Writing.

Copyright © 2000 Ferguson Publishing Company
ISBN 0-89434-318-1

Library of Congress Cataloging-in-Publication Data

Careers in Focus.   Writing
    p.   cm.
  Includes index.
  Summary: Defines the top writing careers in terms of the nature of the work, educational or training requirements, ways to get started, advancement possibilities, salary figures, employment outlook, and sources of more information.
  ISBN 0-89434-318-1
    1. Authorship--Vocational guidance--Juvenile literature. 2. Editing--Vocational guidance--Juvenile literature. I. Title: Writing. II. Ferguson Publishing Company.

PN153.C38 2000
808'.02'2373--dc21

00-021189

Printed in the United States of America

Cover photo courtesy Tony Stone Images

Published and distributed by
Ferguson Publishing Company
200 West Jackson Boulevard, 7th Floor
Chicago, Illinois 60606
800-306-9941
www.fergpubco.com

X-3

Table of Contents

Introduction

Career opportunities for writers can be found not only in publishing, but in film, television, radio, advertising, business and industry, science and medicine, and the arts. And writers are no longer limited to traditional print media—books, magazines, and newspapers. They write for all kinds of media, including the Internet and CD-ROM. Kinds of writing vary from painstakingly technical to wildly creative, from factual to fantastic.

Writers are often behind-the-scenes workers. Most writing careers involve concept development, research, interviewing, collaborating with other workers, as well as the actual crafting of words to be written, spoken, or sung. All writing careers require a love of words and a talent for manipulating language. A few of those careers are presented in this book. Included are jobs in advertising, public relations, music, sports, publishing (books, magazines, and newspapers), radio and television, film, science, and business.

Education requirements for writing jobs vary from a high school diploma to advanced degrees in both writing and an additional specialty. For example, a science writer might be expected to have a degree in biology as well as a journalism degree. Although college-level courses in writing, English, or journalism are highly recommended for most writing positions, many writers start from another career and find they have an ability and liking for writing. A computer software designer might discover on the job that he or she is good at writing computer manuals, or a fund-raiser might find that he or she has a special talent for composing grants.

Salaries for writing careers vary as much as the types of jobs available. A poet may earn only a byline on a published work, while a best-selling novelist may earn millions in fees and royalties. Most writers who work full-time jobs earn between $20,000 and $75,000 a year. Many work on a freelance basis, hiring their services out to one or more clients. They may work for an hourly fee or a per-project fee and these fees may vary according to the job and the employer.

The employment outlook for writers is excellent. Although there is stiff competition for prime writing jobs, there are plenty of opportunities, particularly for those who specialize. Those who want writing careers would do well to have a specialty in addition to sharp writing skills. There will still, however, be jobs for generalists, particularly in newspaper, magazine, and book publishing. Writers who want to pursue a more creative outlet, such as novelist or poet, will encounter the same challenges as they have throughout history—stiff competition, low income, and frequent rejection. Many creative writers, however, hold other full-time writing-related jobs while they work on their more creative pursuits in their spare time.

Each article in this book discusses a particular writing occupation in detail. The information comes from Ferguson's *Encyclopedia of Careers and Vocational Guidance*. The History section describes the history of the particular job as it relates to the overall development of its industry or field. The Job describes the primary and secondary duties of the job. Requirements discusses high school and postsecondary education and training requirements, any certification or licensing necessary, and any other personal requirements for success in the job. Exploring offers suggestions on how to gain some experience in or knowledge of the particular job before making a firm educational and financial commitment. The focus is on what can be done while still in high school (or in the early years of college) to gain a better understanding of the job. The Employers section gives an overview of typical places of employment for the job. Starting Out discusses the best ways to land that first job, be it through the college placement office, newspaper ads, or personal contact. The Advancement section describes what kind of career path to expect from the job and how to get there. Earnings lists salary ranges and describes the typical fringe benefits. The Work Environment section describes the typical surroundings and conditions of employment—whether indoors or outdoors, noisy or quiet, social or independent, and so on. Also discussed are typical hours worked, any seasonal fluctuations, and the stresses and strains of the job. The Outlook section summarizes the job in terms of the general economy and industry projections. For the most part, Outlook information is obtained from the Bureau of Labor Statistics and is supplemented by information taken from professional associations. Job growth terms follow those used in the *Occupational Outlook Handbook*. Growth described as "much faster than the average" means an increase of 36 percent or more. Growth described as "faster than the average" means an increase of 21 to 35 percent. Growth described as "about as fast as the average" means an increase of 10 to 20 percent. Growth described as "little change or more slowly than the average" means an increase of 0 to 9 percent. "Decline" means a decrease of 1 percent or more.

Each article ends with For More Information, which lists organizations that can provide career information on training, education, internships, scholarships, and job placement.

Advertising Workers

	School Subjects
English	
Psychology	

	Personal Skills
Artistic	
Communication/ideas	

	Work Environment
Primarily indoors	
Primarily one location	

	Minimum Education Level
Bachelor's degree	

	Salary Range
$16,000 to $44,000 to $92,000+	

	Certification or Licensing
None available	

	Outlook
About as fast as the average	

Overview

Advertising is defined as mass communication paid for by an advertiser to persuade a particular segment of the public to adopt ideas or take actions of benefit to the advertiser. Advertising workers perform the various creative and business activities needed to take an advertisement from the research stage, to creative concept, through production, and finally to its intended audience. The advertising industry employs 250,000 people at over 20,000 advertising organizations in the United States, including agencies, large corporations, and service and supply houses.

History

Advertising has been around as long as people have been exchanging goods and services. While a number of innovations spurred the development of advertising, it wasn't until the invention of the printing press in the 15th century that merchants began posting handbills in order to advertise their goods and services. By the 19th century, newspapers became an important means of advertising, followed by magazines in the late 1800s.

One of the problems confronting merchants in the early days of advertising was where to place their ads to generate the most business. In response, a number of people emerged who specialized in the area of advertising, accepting ads and posting them conspicuously. These agents were the first advertising workers. As competition among merchants increased, many of these agents offered to compose ads, as well as post them, for their clients.

Today, with intense competition among both new and existing businesses, advertising has become a necessity in the marketing of goods and services alike. At the same time, the advertising worker's job has grown more demanding and complex than ever. With a wide variety of media from which advertisers can choose—including newspapers, magazines, billboards, radio, television, film and video, the World Wide Web, and a variety of other new technologies—today's advertising worker must not only develop and create ads and campaigns but keep abreast of current and developing buying and technology trends as well.

The Job

About seven out of every ten advertising organizations in the United States are full-service operations, offering their clients a broad range of services, including copywriting, graphics and other art-related work, production, media placement, and tracking and follow-up. These advertising agencies may have hundreds of people working in a dozen different departments, while smaller companies often employ just a handful of employees. Most agencies, however, have at least five departments: contact, research, media, creative, and production.

Contact department personnel are responsible for attracting new customers and maintaining relationships with existing ones. Heading the contact department, *advertising agency managers* are concerned with the overall activities of the company. They formulate plans to generate business, by either soliciting new accounts or getting additional business from established clients. In addition, they meet with department heads to coordinate their operations and to create policies and procedures.

Advertising account executives are the contact department employees responsible for maintaining good relations between their clients and the agency. Acting as liaisons, they represent the agency to its clients and must therefore be able to communicate clearly and effectively. After examining clients' advertising objectives, account executives develop campaigns or strategies and then work with others from the various agency departments to target specific audiences, create advertising communications, and execute the campaigns. Presenting concepts, as well as the ad campaign at various stages of completion, to clients for their feedback and approval, account executives must have some knowledge of overall marketing strategies and be able to sell ideas.

Working with account executives, employees in the research department gather, analyze, and interpret the information needed to make a client's advertising campaign successful. By determining who the potential buyers of a product or service will be, *research workers* predict which theme will have the most impact, what kind of packaging and price will have the most appeal, and which media will be the most effective.

Guided by a research director, research workers conduct local, regional, and national surveys in order to examine consumer preferences and then determine potential sales for the targeted product or service based on those preferences. Researchers also gather information about competitors' products, prices, sales, and advertising methods. To learn what the buying public prefers in a client's product over a competitor's, research workers often distribute samples and then ask the users of these samples for their opinions of the product. This information can then be used as testimonials about the product or as a means of identifying the most persuasive selling message in an ad.

Although research workers often recommend which media to use for an advertising campaign, *media planners* are the specialists who determine which print or broadcast media will be the most effective. Ultimately, they are responsible for choosing the combination of media that will reach the greatest number of potential buyers for the least amount of money, based on their clients' advertising strategies. Accordingly, planners must be familiar with the markets that each medium reaches, as well as the advantages and disadvantages of advertising in each.

Media buyers, often referred to as *space buyers* (for newspapers and magazines), or *time buyers* (for radio and television), do the actual purchasing of space and time according to a general plan formulated by the media director. In addition to ensuring that ads appear when and where they should, buyers negotiate costs for ad placement and maintain contact and extensive correspondence with clients and media representatives alike.

While the contact, research, and media departments handle the business side of a client's advertising campaign, the creative staff takes care of the artistic aspects. *Creative directors* oversee the activities of artists and writers and work with clients and account executives to determine the best advertising approaches, gain approval on concepts, and establish budgets and schedules.

Copywriters take the ideas submitted by creative directors and account executives and write descriptive text in the form of headlines, jingles, slogans, and other copy designed to attract the attention of potential buyers. In addition to being able to express themselves clearly and persuasively, copywriters must know what motivates people to buy. They must also be able to describe a product's features in a captivating and appealing way and be familiar with various advertising media. In large agencies, copywriters may be supervised by a copy chief.

Copywriters work closely with art directors to make sure that text and artwork create a unified, eye-catching arrangement. Planning the visual presentation of the client's message—from concept formulation to final artwork—the art director plays an important role in every stage of the creation of an advertising campaign. Art directors who work on filmed commercials and videos combine film techniques, music, and sound, as well as actors or animation, to communicate an advertiser's message. In publishing, art directors work with graphic designers, photographers, copywriters, and editors to develop brochures, catalogs, direct mail, and other printed pieces, all according to the advertising strategy.

Art directors must have a basic knowledge of graphics and design, computer software, printing, photography, and filmmaking. With the help of graphic artists, they decide where to place text and images, choose typefaces, and storyboard ads and videos. Several layouts are usually submitted to the client, who chooses one or asks for revisions until a layout or conceptualization sketch meets with final approval. The art director then selects an illustrator, graphic artist, photographer, or TV or video producer, and the project moves on to the production department of the agency.

Production departments in large ad agencies may be divided into print production and broadcast production divisions, each with its own managers and staff. *Production managers* and their assistants convert and reproduce written copy and artwork into printed, filmed, or tape-recorded form so that they can be presented to the public. *Production employees* work closely with imaging, printing, engraving, and other art reproduction firms and must be familiar with various printing processes, papers, inks, typography, still and motion picture photography, digital imaging, and other processes and materials.

In addition to the principle employees in the five major departments, advertising organizations work with a variety of staff or freelance employees who have specialized knowledge, education, and skill, including photographers, photoengravers, typographers, printers, telemarketers, product and package designers, and producers of display materials. Finally, rounding out most advertising establishments are various support employees, such as production coordinators, video editors, word processors, statisticians, accountants, administrators, secretaries, and clerks.

The work of advertising employees is fast-paced, dynamic, and ever-changing, depending on each client's strategies and budgets and the creative ideas generated by agency workers. In addition to innovative techniques, methods, media, and materials used by agency workers, new and emerging technologies are impacting the work of everyone in the advertising arena, from marketing executives to graphic designers. The Internet is undoubtedly the most revolutionary medium to hit the advertising scene. Through this worldwide, computer-based network, researchers are able to precisely target markets and clearly identify consumer needs. In addition, the Internet's Web pages provide media specialists with a powerful vehicle for advertising their clients' products and services. New technology has also been playing an important role in the creative area. Most art directors, for example, use a variety of computer software programs, and many create and oversee Web sites for their clients. Other interactive materials and vehicles, such as CD catalogs, touch-screens, multidimensional visuals, and voice-mail shopping, are changing the way today's advertising workers are doing their jobs.

Requirements

High School

The many kinds of advertising workers have varied educational and experiential backgrounds that defy a single set of qualifications. As a general rule, most advertising positions require a bachelor's degree; in some cases, however, it is not absolutely necessary. The creative department, for example, does not require a bachelor's degree for most entry-level positions. While having a college degree gives candidates a competitive edge, advertising establishments do not require them of their assistant copywriters. Similarly, TV producers and production department workers are less likely to need a college degree than those in other agency positions. Assistant art directors, however, usually must have at least a two-year degree from a design or art school.

You can prepare for a career as an advertising worker by taking a variety of courses at the high school level. General liberal arts courses, such as English, journalism, communication, economics, psychology, business, social science, and mathematics, are important for aspiring advertising employees. In addition, those interested in the creative side of the field should take such classes as art, drawing, graphic design, illustration, and art history. Finally, since computers play a vital role in the advertising field, you should become familiar with word processing and layout programs, as well as the World Wide Web.

Postsecondary Training

The American Association of Advertising Agencies notes that most agencies employing entry-level personnel prefer college graduates. Copywriters are best prepared with a college degree in English, journalism, or communications; research workers need college training in statistics, market research, and social studies; and most account executives have business or related degrees. Media positions are increasingly requiring a college degree in communications or a technology-related area. Media directors and research directors with a master's degree have a distinct advantage over those with only an undergraduate degree. Some research department heads even have doctorates.

While the requirements from agency to agency may vary somewhat, graduates of liberal arts colleges or those with majors in fields such as communications, journalism, business administration, or marketing research are preferred. Good language skills, as well as a broad liberal arts background, are necessary for advertising workers. College students interested in the field should therefore take such courses as English, writing, art, philosophy, foreign languages, social studies, sociology, psychology, economics, mathematics, statistics, advertising, and marketing. Some 900 degree-granting institutions throughout the United States offer specialized majors in advertising as part of their curriculum.

Other Requirements

In addition to the variety of educational and work experiences necessary for those aspiring to advertising careers, many personal characteristics are also important. Although advertising employees perform many tasks of their jobs independently, most interact with others as part of a team. In addition to working with other staff members, many advertising workers are responsible for initiating and maintaining client contact. They must therefore be able to get along well with people and communicate clearly.

Advertising is not a job that involves routine, and workers must be able to meet and adjust to the challenges presented by each new client and product or service. The ability to think clearly and logically is important, because commonsense approaches rather than gimmicks persuade people that something is worth buying. Advertising workers must also be creative, flexible, and imaginative in order to anticipate consumer demand and trends, to develop effective concepts, and to sell the ideas, products, and services of their clients.

Finally, with technology evolving at breakneck speed, it's vital for advertising workers to keep pace with technological advances and trends. In addition to being able to work with the most current software and hardware, employees should be familiar with the Web, as well as with other technology that is impacting—and will continue to impact—the industry.

Exploring

For those aspiring to jobs in the advertising industry, some insight can be gained by taking writing and art courses offered either in school or by private organizations. In addition to the theoretical ideas and techniques that such classes can provide, you can actually apply what you learn by working full- or part-time at local department stores or newspaper offices. Some advertising agencies or research firms also employ students to interview people or to conduct other market research. Work as an agency clerk or messenger may also be available. Participating in internships at an advertising or marketing organization is yet another way to explore the field, as well as to determine your aptitude for advertising work.

Employers

Most advertising workers are employed by advertising agencies that plan and prepare advertising material for their clients on a commission or service fee basis. However, some large companies and nearly all department stores prefer to handle their own advertising. Advertising workers in such organizations prepare advertising materials for in-house clients, such as the marketing or catalog department. They also may be involved in the planning, preparation, and production of special promotional materials, such as sales brochures, articles describing the activities of the organization, or Web sites. Some advertising workers are employed by owners of various media, including newspapers, magazines, radio and television networks, and outdoor advertising. Workers employed in these media are mainly sales representatives who sell advertising space or broadcast time to advertising agencies or companies that maintain their own advertising departments.

In addition to agencies, large companies, and department stores, advertising services and supply houses employ such advertising specialists as photographers, photoengravers, typographers, printers, product and package designers, display producers, and others who assist in the production of various advertising materials.

Of the 22,000 advertising agencies in the United States, most of the large firms are located in Chicago, Los Angeles, and New York. Employment opportunities are also available, however, at a variety of "small shops," four out of five of which employ fewer than 10 workers each. In addition, a growing number of self-employment and home-based business opportunities is resulting in a variety of industry jobs located in outlying areas rather than in big cities.

Starting Out

Although competition for advertising jobs is fierce and getting your foot in the door can be difficult, there is a variety of ways to launch a career in the field. Some large advertising agencies recruit college graduates and place them in training programs designed to acquaint beginners with all aspects of advertising work, but these opportunities are limited and highly competitive.

Instead, many graduates simply send resumes to businesses that employ entry-level advertising workers. Newspapers, radio and television stations, printers, photographers, and advertising agencies are but a few of the businesses that will hire beginners. *The Standard Directory of Advertising Agencies* lists the names and addresses of ad agencies all across the nation. You can find the directory in almost any public library.

Those who have had work experience in sales positions often enter the advertising field as account executives. High school graduates and other people without experience who want to work in advertising, however, may find it necessary to begin as clerks or assistants to research and production staff members or to copywriters.

Advancement

The career path in an advertising agency generally leads from trainee to skilled worker to division head and then to department head. It may also take employees from department to department, allowing them to gain more responsibility with each move. Opportunities abound for those with talent, leadership capability, and ambition.

Management positions require experience in all aspects of advertising, including agency work, communication with advertisers, and knowledge of various advertising media. Copywriters, account executives, and other advertising agency workers who demonstrate outstanding ability to deal with clients and supervise coworkers usually have a good chance of advancing to management positions. Other workers, however, prefer to acquire specialized skills. For them, advancement may mean more responsibility, the opportunity to perform more specialized tasks, and increased pay.

Advertising workers at various department stores, mail order houses, and other large firms that have their own advertising departments can also earn promotions. Advancement in any phase of advertising work is usually dependent on the employee's experience, training, and demonstrated skills.

Some qualified copywriters, artists, and account executives establish their own agencies or become marketing consultants. For these entrepreneurs, advancement may take the form of an increasing number of accounts and/or more prestigious clients.

Earnings

Salaries of advertising workers vary depending on the type of work, the size of the agency, its geographic location, the kind of accounts handled, and the agency's gross earnings. Salaries are also determined by a worker's education, aptitude, and experience. The wide range of jobs in advertising makes it difficult to estimate average salaries for all positions. Entry-level jobs, of course, may pay considerably less than the figures given in the following paragraphs.

In advertising agencies, chief executives can earn from $80,000 annually, upwards to $750,000, while experienced account executives average $44,000 a year or more. In the research and media departments, research directors average $61,000 annually, experienced analysts up to $51,800 per year, media directors between $46,000 and $92,400 annually, and media planners and buyers $27,500 to $32,500 per year. In the creative department, copywriters earn, on average, $56,000 per year, art directors between

$44,500 to $60,000 or more annually, and creative directors $92,000 per year. Finally, production managers make about $31,000 per year.

In other businesses and industries, individual earnings vary widely. Salaries of advertising workers are generally higher, however, at consumer product firms than at industrial product organizations because of the competition among consumer product producers. The majority of companies offer insurance benefits, a retirement plan, and other incentives and bonuses.

Work Environment

Conditions at most agencies are similar to those found in other offices throughout the country, except that employees must frequently work under great pressure to meet deadlines. While a traditional 40-hour workweek is the norm at some companies, one-third of the advertising industry's full-time employees report that they work 50 hours or more per week, including evenings and weekends. Bonuses and time off during slow periods are sometimes provided as a means of compensation for unusual workloads and hours.

Although some advertising employees, such as researchers, work independently on a great many tasks, most must function as part of a team. With frequent meetings with coworkers, clients, and media representatives alike, the work environment is usually energized, with ideas being exchanged, contracts being negotiated, and schedules being modified.

Advertising work is fast-paced and exciting. As a result, many employees often feel stressed out as they are constantly challenged to take initiative and be creative. Nevertheless, advertising workers enjoy both professional and personal satisfaction in seeing the culmination of their work communicated to sometimes millions of people.

Outlook

Employment opportunities in the advertising field are expected to increase about as fast as the average for all industries through the year 2006. Demand for advertising workers will grow as a result of increased production of goods and services, both in the United States and abroad. Network television, cable, radio, newspapers, the Web, and other media (particularly interactive vehicles) will offer advertising workers an increasing number of employment opportunities. Other media, such as magazines, direct mail, and event marketing, are expected to provide fewer job opportunities.

Advertising agencies will enjoy faster than average employment growth, as will industries that service ad agencies and other businesses in the advertising field, such as those that offer commercial photography, imaging, art, and graphics services.

At the two extremes, enormous "mega-agencies" and small shops employing up to only 10 workers each offer employment opportunities for people with experience, talent, flexibility, and drive. In addition, self-employment and home-based businesses are on the rise. Many nonindustrial companies, such as banks, schools, and hospitals, will also be creating advertising positions through the end of the century.

In general, openings will become available to replace workers who change positions, retire, or leave the field for other reasons. Competition for these jobs will be keen, however, because of the large number of qualified professionals in this traditionally desirable field. Opportunities will be best for the well-qualified and well-trained applicant. Employers favor those who are college graduates with experience, a high level of creativity, and strong communications skills. People who are not well qualified or prepared for agency work will find the advertising field increasingly difficult to enter. The same is also true for those who seek work in companies that service ad agencies.

For More Information

The AAF is the professional advertising association that binds the mutual interests of corporate advertisers, agencies, media companies, suppliers, and academia.

American Advertising Federation
1101 Vermont Avenue, NW, Suite 500
Washington, DC 20005-6306
Tel: 202-898-0089
Web: http://www.aaf.org

The AAAA is the management-oriented national trade organization representing the advertising agency business.

American Association of Advertising Agencies
405 Lexington, 18th Floor
New York, NY 10174-1801
Tel: 212-682-2500
Web: http://www.aaaa.org/

The AMA is an international professional society of individual members with an interest in the practice, study, and teaching of marketing.

American Marketing Association
250 South Wacker Drive, Suite 200
Chicago, IL 60606
Tel: 312-648-0536
Web: http://ama.org

The Art Directors Club is an international, nonprofit organization for creatives in advertising, graphic design, interactive media, broadcast design, typography, packaging, environmental design, photography, illustration, and related disciplines.

Art Directors Club
250 Park Avenue South
New York, NY 10003
Tel: 212-674-0500
Web: http://www.adcny.org

The DMA is the largest trade association for individuals interested in database marketing.

Direct Marketing Association
1120 Avenue of the Americas
New York, NY 10036-6700
Tel: 212-768-7277
Web: http://www.the-dma.org

The Graphic Artists Guild promotes and protects the economic interests of the artist/designer and is committed to improving conditions for all creators of graphic art and raising standards for the entire industry.

Graphic Artists Guild
90 Johns Street, Suite 403
New York, NY 10038-3202
Tel: 212-791-3400
Web: http://www.gag.org

Book Editors

	School Subjects
Computer science English	
	Personal Skills
Artistic Communication/ideas	
	Work Environment
Primarily indoors Primarily one location	
	Minimum Education Level
Bachelor's degree	
	Salary Range
$18,000 to $25,000 to $42,500	
	Certification or Licensing
None available	
	Outlook
Faster than the average	

Overview

Book editors acquire and prepare written material for publication in book form. Such formats include trade books (fiction and nonfiction), textbooks, and technical and professional books (which include reference books). A book editor's duties include evaluating a manuscript, accepting or rejecting it, rewriting, correcting spelling and grammar, researching, and fact checking. Book editors may work directly with printers in arranging for proofs and with artists and designers in arranging for illustration matter and determining the physical specifications of the book. (Also see *Editors*.)

In 1996, more than 90,000 editors and writers worked for newspapers, magazines, and book publishers. Book editors are employed at small and large publishing houses, book packagers (companies that specialize in book production), associations, and government agencies.

The Job

The editorial department is generally the main core of any publishing house. Procedures and terminology may vary from one type of publishing house to another, but there is some general agreement among the essentials. Publishers of trade books, textbooks, and reference books all have somewhat different needs for which they have developed different editorial practices.

The editor has the principal responsibility in evaluating the manuscript. The editor responsible for seeing a book through to publication may hold any of several titles. The highest level editorial executive in a publishing house is usually the editor in chief or editorial director. The person holding either of these titles directs the overall operation of the editorial department. Sometimes an executive editor occupies the highest position in an editorial department. The next level of editor is often the managing editor, who keeps track of schedules and deadlines and must know where all manuscripts are at any given time. Other editors who handle copy include the senior editors, associate editors, assistant editors, editorial assistants, and copy editors.

In a trade-book house, the editor, usually at the senior or associate position, works with manuscripts that he or she has solicited from authors or that have been submitted by known authors or their agents. Editors who seek out authors to write manuscripts are also known as acquisitions editors.

In technical/professional book houses, editors commonly do more researching, revising, and rewriting than trade-book editors do. These editors are often required to be skilled in certain subjects. Editors must be sure that the subject is comprehensively covered and organized according to an agreed-upon outline. Editors contract for virtually all of the material that comes into technical/professional book houses. The authors they solicit are often scholars.

Editors who edit heavily or ask an author to revise extensively must learn to be highly diplomatic; the art of author-editor relations is a critical aspect of the editor's job.

When the editor is satisfied with the manuscript, it goes to the copy editor. The copy editor usually does the final editing of the manuscript before it goes to the typesetter. On almost any type of manuscript, the copy editor is responsible for correcting errors of spelling, punctuation, grammar, and usage.

The copy editor marks up the manuscript to indicate where different kinds of typefaces are used and where charts, illustrations, and photos may be inserted. It is important for the copy editor to discover any inconsistencies in the text and to query the author about them. The copy editor then usually acts as a liaison between the typesetter, the editor, and the author as the manuscript is typeset into galley proofs and then page proofs.

In a small house, one editor might do the work of all of the editors described here. There can also be separate fact checkers, proofreaders, style editors, also called line editors, and indexers. An assistant editor could be assigned to do many of the kinds of jobs handled by the senior or associate editors. Editorial assistants provide support for the other editors and may be required to proofread and handle some administrative duties.

Requirements

Postsecondary Training

A college degree is a requirement for entry into the field of book editing. For general editing, a degree in English or journalism is particularly valuable, although most degrees in the liberal arts are acceptable. Degrees in other fields, such as the sciences, psychology, mathematics, or applied arts, can be useful in publishing houses that produce books related to those fields. Textbook and technical/professional book houses in particular seek out editors with strengths in certain subject areas. Whatever the type of degree, the aspiring book editor needs an education with considerable emphasis on writing and communications courses.

Other Requirements

Book editors need a sharp eye for detail and a compulsion for accuracy. Intellectual curiosity, self-motivation, and a respect for deadlines are important characteristics for book editors. Knowledge of word processing and desktop publishing programs is necessary.

It goes without saying that if you are seeking a career in book editing, you not only love to read, but love books for their own sake as well. If you are not an avid reader, you are not likely to go far as a book editor. The craft and history of bookmaking itself is also something in which a young book editor should be interested. A keen interest in any subject, be it a sport, a hobby, or an avocation, can lead one into special areas of book publishing.

Employers

Book editors may find employment with small publishing houses, large publishing houses, the federal government, or book packagers, or they may be self-employed as freelancers. The major book publishers are located in larger cities, such as New York, Chicago, Los Angeles, Boston, Philadelphia, San Francisco, and Washington, DC. Publishers of professional, religious, business, and technical books are dispersed throughout the country.

Earnings

A salary survey published in *Publishers Weekly* in July of 1998 stated that editorial salaries were definitely tied to the size of the publishing company. Salaries for entry-level jobs, such as editorial assistant, range from $25,000 to $45,000. Editors in more advanced positions earn from $52,000 to $53,800 annually. The annual salary for supervisory editors ranges from $43,300 to $88,700.

Publishers usually offer employee benefits that are about average for U.S. industry. There are other benefits, however. Most editors enjoy working with people who like books, and the atmosphere of an editorial department is generally intellectual and stimulating. Some book editors have the opportunity to travel—to attend meetings, to meet with authors, or to do research.

Outlook

Most editing jobs will continue to be competitive through the year 2006, and employment is expected to increase faster than average, according to the *Occupational Outlook Handbook*. The growth of online publishing will increase the need for editors who are Web experts. Turnover is relatively high in publishing—editors often advance by moving to another firm or by establishing a freelance business. There are many publishers and organizations that operate with a minimal salaried staff and hire freelance editors for everything from project management to proofreading and production.

For More Information

Literary Market Place, published annually by R. R. Bowker, lists the names of publishing companies in the United States and Canada as well as their specialties and the names of their key personnel. For additional information about careers in publishing, contact the following:

Association of American Publishers
71 Fifth Avenue
New York, NY 10003-3004
Tel: 212-255-0200
Web: http://www.publishers.org

Florida Publishers Association (Independent Publishers)
PO Box 430
Highland City, FL 33846-0430
Tel: 941-647-5951
Web: http://www.flbookpub.org/

Columnists

Overview

Columnists write opinion pieces for publication in newspapers or magazines. Some columnists work for syndicates—organizations that sell articles to many media at once.

Columnists can be generalists who write about whatever strikes them on any topic. Most columnists focus on a specialty, such as government, politics, local issues, health, humor, sports, gossip, or other themes.

Most newspapers employ local columnists or run columns from syndicates. Some syndicated columnists work out of their homes or private offices.

History

Because the earliest American newspapers were political vehicles, much of their news stories brimmed with commentary and opinion. This practice continued up until the Civil War. Horace Greeley, one of the most read of the editors who had regularly espoused partisanship in his *New York Tribune,* was the first to give editorial opinion its own page separate from the news.

As newspapers grew into instruments of mass communication, their editors sought balance and fairness on the editorial pages and began publishing a number of columns with varying viewpoints.

Famous Washington, DC-based columnist Jack Anderson is known for bringing an investigative slant to the editorial page. Art Buchwald and Molly Ivins became well known for their satirical look at government and politicians.

The growth of news and commentary on the Internet has only added to the power of columnists.

The Job

Columnists take a news story and enhance the facts with personal opinion and panache. Or a column may be based on personal experience. Either way, a column usually has a punchy start, a pithy middle, and a strong, sometimes poignant, ending.

Columnists are responsible for writing columns on a regular basis in accord with a schedule, depending on the frequency of publication. It may be that they write a column daily, weekly, quarterly, or monthly. Like other journalists, they face pressure to meet a deadline.

Most columnists are free to select their own story ideas. The need to constantly come up with new ideas may be one of the hardest parts of the job, but also one of the most rewarding. Columnists search through newspapers, magazines, and the Internet, watch television, and listen to the radio. The various types of media suggest ideas, and keep the writer aware of current events and social issues.

Next they do research, delving into a topic much like an investigative reporter would, so that they can back up their arguments with facts.

Finally, they write, usually on a computer. After a column is written, at least one editor goes over it to check for clarity and correct mistakes. Then the cycle begins again. Often a columnist will write a few relatively timeless pieces to keep for use as backups in a pinch, in case a new idea can't be found or falls through.

Most columnists work in newsrooms or magazine offices, although some, especially those who are syndicated but not affiliated with a particular newspaper, work out of their homes or private offices. Many well-known syndicated columnists work out of Washington, DC.

Newspapers often run small pictures of columnists, called head shots, next to their columns. This, and a consistent placement of a column in a particular spot in the paper, usually gives a columnist greater recognition than a reporter or editor.

Requirements

High School

High school students should take English and writing classes and participate in extracurricular activities such as the school newspaper or debate team.

Postsecondary Training

As is the case for other journalists, at least a bachelor's degree in journalism is usually required, although some journalists graduate with degrees in political science or English. Experience may be gained by writing for the college or university newspaper, and through a summer internship at a newspaper or other publication. It also may be helpful to submit freelance opinion columns to local or national publications. The more published articles, called "clips," graduates can show to prospective employers, the better.

Other Requirements

To be a columnist requires similar characteristics as those for being a reporter: curiosity, a genuine interest in people, ability to write clearly and succinctly, and the strength to thrive under deadline pressure. But columnists also require a certain wit and wisdom, the compunction to express strong opinions, and the ability to take apart an issue and debate it.

Exploring

A good way to explore this career is to work for your school newspaper and perhaps write your own column. Participation in debate clubs will help you form opinions and express them clearly

Employers

Newspapers of all kinds run columns, as do certain magazines and even public radio stations, where a tape is played over the airways of the author reading the column. Some columnists are self-employed, preferring to market their work to syndicates instead of working for a single newspaper or magazine.

Starting Out

Most columnists start out as reporters. Experienced reporters are the ones most likely to become columnists. Occasionally, however, a relatively new reporter may suggest a weekly column if the beat being covered warrants it, for example, politics.

Another route is to start out by freelancing, sending columns out to a multitude of newspapers and magazines in the hopes that someone will pick them up. Also, columns can be marketed to syndicates. A list of these, and magazines that may also be interested in columns, is provided in the *Writer's Market*.

Advancement

Newspaper columnists can advance in national exposure by having their work syndicated. Or they may try to get a collection of their columns published in book form.

Columnists also may choose other editorial positions, such as editor, editorial writer or page editor, or foreign correspondent.

Earnings

Like reporters' salaries, the incomes of columnists vary greatly according to experience, newspaper size and location, and whether the columnist is under a union contract. But generally, columnists make higher salaries than reporters.

Average starting salaries for writers, including columnists, was about $20,000 in 1997, according to the Dow Jones Newspaper Fund. After several years of experience, columnists can make top salaries of $60,000 or more a year.

Freelancers may get paid by the column. Syndicates pay columnists 40 percent to 60 percent of the sales income generated by their columns or a flat fee if only one column is being sold.

Work Environment

Columnists work mostly indoors in newspaper or magazine offices, although they may occasionally conduct interviews or do research on location out of the office. Some columnists may work as much as 48 to 52 hours a week.

Outlook

The number of newspaper reporter jobs is projected to decrease in coming years, but the number of magazine writer jobs is expected to increase. Probably, like foreign correspondents, the number of columnists will remain fairly stable. If a newspaper is small, or falls on hard times, managing editors may expect a local columnist to also take on reporting duties. Competition for newspaper jobs is stiff, and for columnist positions, even stiffer, because they are highly prized among reporters and because there are so few of them. Smaller daily and weekly newspapers may be easier places to find employment than major metropolitan newspapers, and movement up the ladder to columnist will also likely be quicker, but the pay is less than at bigger papers. New publications on the Internet also may be good places to start.

For More Information

The ASJA provides information on careers in newspaper reporting, as well as information on education and financial aid.

American Society of Journalists and Authors
1501 Broadway, Suite 302
New York, NY 10036
Tel: 212-997-0947
Email: 75227.1650@compuserve.com
Web: http://www.asja.org/cw950615.htm

The AEJMC provides general educational information on all areas of journalism (newspapers, magazines, television, and radio).

Association for Education in Journalism and Mass Communication
121 LaConte College
University of South Carolina
Columbia, SC 29208-0251
Tel: 803-777-2006
Email: aejmc@sc.edu
Web: http://www.aejmc.sc.edu/on-line/home.html

The NAB has information on jobs, scholarships, internships, college programs, and other resources. It offers **Careers in Radio** *($4) and* **Careers in Television** *($4), which describe the key jobs, educational requirements, and job-related experience required.*

National Association of Broadcasters
1771 N Street, NW
Washington, DC 20036
Tel: 202-429-5300
Email: jearnhar@nab.org
Web: http://www.nab.org

The SPJ has student chapters all over the United States. Among its many services to students, it offers information on scholarships and internships.

Society of Professional Journalists
16 South Jackson
Greencastle, IN 46135-0077
Tel: 765-653-3333
Email: spj@spjhq.org
Web: http://www.spj.org

Desktop Publishing Specialists

	School Subjects
Art Computer science English	
	Personal Skills
Artistic Communication/ideas	
	Work Environment
Primarily one location Primarily indoors	
	Minimum Education Level
High school diploma	
	Salary Range
$18,000 to $30,000 to $83,000	
	Certification or Licensing
Voluntary	
	Outlook
Faster than the average	

Overview

Desktop publishing specialists prepare reports, brochures, books, cards, and other documents for printing. They create computer files of text, graphics, and page layout. They work with files others have created, or they compose original text and graphics for the client. There are around 50,000 desktop publishing specialists working in the printing industry, either as freelancers or for corporations, service bureaus, and advertising agencies.

History

When Johannes Gutenberg invented movable type in the 1440s, it seemed like a major technological advancement. Up until that point, books were produced entirely by hand by monks, every word written in ink on vellum.

Though print shops flourished all across Europe with this invention, inspiring the production of millions of books by the 1500s, there was no other major change in the technology of printing until the 1800s. By then, cylinder presses were churning out thousands of sheets per hour, and the Linotype machine allowed for easier, more efficient plate-making. Offset lithography (a method of applying ink from a treated surface onto paper) followed and gained popularity after World War II. Phototypesetting was later developed, involving creating film images of text and pictures to be printed. At the end of the 20th century, computers caused another revolution in the industry. Laser printers now allow for low-cost, high-quality printing, and desktop publishing software is credited with spurring sales and use of personal home computers.

The Job

If you've ever used a computer to design and print flyers to promote a high school play, or if you've put together a small literary magazine, then you've had some experience in desktop publishing. Not so many years ago, the prepress process (the steps to prepare a document for the printing press) involved metal casts, molten lead, light tables, knives, wax, paste, and a number of different professionals from artists to typesetters. With computer technology, these jobs are becoming more consolidated. A desktop publishing specialist is someone with artistic talents, proofreading skills, sales and marketing abilities, and a great deal of computer knowledge. As a desktop publishing specialist, you'll work on computers converting and preparing files for printing presses and other media, such as the Internet and CD-ROM. Much of desktop publishing fits into the prepress category, and desktop publishing specialists typeset, or arrange and transform, text and graphics. Your work is performed at a home computer using the latest in design software. Macintosh programs such as FreeHand, Illustrator, and PageMaker, are the most popular with desktop publishing specialists, though PC programs like Corel Draw and PhotoShop are also gaining popularity. Some desktop publishing specialists use CAD (computer-aided design) technology, allowing them to create images and effects with a digitizing pen.

Once you've created the file to be printed, you'll either submit it to a commercial printer, or you'll print the pieces yourself. Whereas traditional typesetting costs over $20 per page, desktop printing can cost less than a penny a page. Individuals hire the services of desktop publishing specialists for creating and printing invitations, advertising and fundraising brochures, newsletters, flyers, and business cards. Commercial printing involves catalogs, brochures, and reports, while business printing encompasses products used by businesses, such as sales receipts and forms.

Typesetting and page layout work entails selecting font types and sizes, arranging column widths, checking for proper spacing between letters, words, and columns, placing graphics and pictures, and more. You'll choose from the hundreds of typefaces available, taking the purpose and tone of the text into consideration when selecting from fonts with round shapes or long shapes, thick strokes or thin, serifs or sans serifs. Editing is also an important duty of a desktop publishing specialist. Articles must be updated, or in some cases rewritten, before they can be arranged on a page. As more people use their own desktop publishing programs to create print-ready files, you'll have to be skillful at designing original work, and promoting your talents, in order to remain competitive.

Darryl Gabriel and his wife Maree own a desktop publishing service in Australia—the Internet has allowed them to publicize the business globally. They currently serve customers in their local area and across Australia, and are hoping to expand more into international Internet marketing. Darryl and Maree use a computer ("But one is not enough," Darryl says), a laser printer, and a scanner to create business cards, pamphlets, labels, books, and personalized greeting cards. Though they must maintain computer skills, they also have a practical understanding of the equipment. "We keep our prices down by being able to re-ink our cartridges," Darryl says. "This takes a little getting used to at first, but once you get a knack for it, it becomes easier."

You'll be dealing with technical issues, such as resolution problems, colors that need to be corrected, and software difficulties, but you'll also use creativity and artistic skills to create designs. Many of your clients will bring you graphics they've designed themselves using computer software programs, while others will bring you drawings in pencil and paper. They provide you with their designs, and you must convert these designs to the format requested by the designers. A designer may come in with a hand-drawn sketch, a printout of a design, or a file on a diskette, and he or she may want the design to be ready for publication on the World Wide Web, in a high-quality brochure, or in a newspaper or magazine. Each format presents different issues, and you must be familiar with the processes and solutions for each. You may also provide services such as color scanning, laminating, image manipulation, and poster production.

Customer relations are as important as technical skills. Darryl emphasizes the importance of learning how to use your equipment and software to their fullest potential, but he also advises you to know your customers. "Try and be as helpful as possible to your customers," he says, "so you can provide them with products that they are happy with and that are going to benefit their businesses." He says it's also very important to follow up, calling customers to make sure they're pleased with the work. "If you're able to relate to what the customers want, and if you encourage them to be involved in the initial design process, then they'll be confident they're going to get quality products."

Requirements

High School

Classes that will help you develop desktop publishing skills include computer classes and design and art classes. Computer classes should include both hardware and software, since understanding how computers function will help you with troubleshooting and knowing the computer's limits. In photography classes you can learn about composition, color, and design elements. Typing, drafting, and print shop classes, if available, will also provide you with the opportunity to gain some indispensable skills. Working on the school newspaper or yearbook will train you on desktop publishing skills as well, including page layout, typesetting, composition, and working under a deadline.

Postsecondary Training

Although a college degree is not a prerequisite, many desktop publishing specialists have at least a bachelor's degree. Areas of study range anywhere from English and communications, to graphic design. Some two-year colleges and technical institutes offer programs in desktop publishing or related fields. A growing number of schools offer programs in technical and visual communications, which may include classes in desktop publishing, layout and design, and computer graphics. Four-year colleges also offer courses in technical communications and graphic design. There are many opportunities to take classes related to desktop publishing through extended education programs offered through universities and colleges. These classes can range from basic desktop publishing techniques to advanced courses in Adobe Photoshop or QuarkXPress and are often taught by professionals working in the industry.

A number of professional organizations and schools offer scholarship and grant opportunities. The Graphic Arts Education and Research Foundation (GAERF) and the Education Council of the Graphic Arts

Industry, Inc., both divisions of the Association for Suppliers of Printing and Publishing Technologies (NPES), can provide information on scholarship opportunities and research grants. Other organizations that offer financial awards and information on scholarship opportunities include the Society for Technical Communication, the International Prepress Association, the Printing Industries of America (PIA), and the Graphic Arts Technical Foundation, which offers scholarships in graphic communications through the National Scholarship Trust Fund.

Certification or Licensing

Certification is not mandatory, and currently there is only one certification program offered in desktop publishing. The Association of Graphic Communications has an Electronic Publishing Certificate designed to set industry standards and measure the competency levels of desktop publishing specialists. The examination is divided into a written portion and a hands-on portion. During the practical portion of the examination, candidates receive files on a disk and must manipulate images and text, make color corrections, and perform whatever tasks are necessary to create the final product. Applicants are expected to be knowledgeable in print production, color separation, typography and font management, computer hardware and software, image manipulation, page layout, scanning and color correcting, prepress and preflighting, and output device capabilities.

PIA is in the process of developing industry standards in the prepress and press industries. PIA may eventually design a certification program in desktop publishing or electronic prepress operation.

Other Requirements

Desktop publishing specialists are detail-oriented, possess problem-solving skills, and have a sense of design and artistic skills. "People tell me I have a flair for graphic design," Darryl says, "and mixing the right color with the right graphics." A good eye and patience are critical, as well as endurance to see projects through to the finish. You should have an aptitude for computers, the ability to type quickly and accurately, and a natural curiosity. A calm temperament comes in handy when working under pressure and constant deadlines. You should be flexible and be able to handle more than one project at a time.

Exploring

Experimenting with your home computer, or a computer at school or the library, will give you a good idea as to whether desktop publishing is for you. Play around with various graphic design and page layout programs. If you subscribe to an Internet service, take advantage of any free Web space available to you and design your own home page. Join computer clubs and volunteer at small organizations to produce newsletters and flyers; volunteering is an excellent way to try new software and techniques, and to gain experience troubleshooting and creating final products. Also, part-time or summer employment with printing shops and companies that have in-house publishing or printing departments are great ways to gain experience and make valuable contacts.

Employers

Your clients will include individuals and small business owners, such as publishing houses, advertising agencies, graphic design agencies, and printing shops. Some large companies also contract with desktop publishing services, rather than hire full-time staffs of designers. Government agencies hire desktop publishing specialists for the large number of documents they publish. The Government Printing Office (GPO) has a Digital Information Technology Support Group (DITS Group) that provides desktop and electronic publishing services to federal agencies.

You'll usually be dealing directly with your clients, but in some cases you may be subcontracting work from printers, designers, and other desktop publishing specialists. You may also hire your services as a consultant, working with printing professionals to help solve particular design problems.

Starting Out

To start your own business, you must have a great deal of experience with design and page layout, and a careful understanding of the computer design programs you'll be using. Before striking out on your own, you may want to gain experience as a full-time staff member of a large business. Most desktop publishing specialists enter the field through the production side, or the editorial side of the industry. Those with training as a designer or artist can easily master the finer techniques of production. Printing houses and design agencies are places to check for production artist opportunities. Publishing companies often hire desktop publishing specialists to work in-house or as freelance employees. Working within the industry, you can make connections and build up a clientele.

You can also start out by investing in computer hardware and software, and volunteering your services. By designing logos, letterhead, and restaurant menus, your work will gain quick recognition, and word of your services will spread.

Advancement

The growth of Darryl and Maree's business is requiring that they invest in another computer and printer. "We want to expand," Darryl says, "develop with technology, and venture into Internet marketing and development. We also intend to be a thorn in the side of the larger commercial printing businesses in town." In addition to taking on more print projects, you can expand your business into Web design and page layout for Internet magazines.

Earnings

There is limited salary information available for desktop publishing specialists, most likely because the job duties of desktop publishing specialists can vary and often overlap with other jobs. According to a salary survey conducted by PIA in 1997, the average wage of desktop publishing specialists in the prepress department ranged from $11.72 to $14.65 an hour, with the highest rate at $40 an hour. Entry-level desktop publishing specialists with little or no experience generally earn minimum wage. Electronic page make-up system operators earned an average of $13.62 to $16.96, and scanner operators ranged from $14.89 to $17.91.

According to the 1998-99 *Occupational Outlook Handbook,* full-time prepress workers in typesetting and composition earned a median wage of $421 a week, or $21,892 annually. Wage rates vary depending on experience, training, region, and size of the company.

Work Environment

Desktop publishing specialists spend most of their time working in front of a computer, whether editing text, or laying out pages. They need to be able to work with other prepress operators, and deal with clients. Hours may vary depending on project deadlines at hand. Some projects may take one day to complete, while others may take a week or longer. Projects may range from designing a logo for letterhead, preparing a catalog for the printer, or working on a file that will be published on the World Wide Web.

Outlook

According to the 1998-99 *Occupational Outlook Handbook,* the field of desktop publishing is projected to be one of the fastest growing occupations, increasing about 75 percent through the year 2006. In 1996, there were a total of 30,000 desktop publishing specialists employed in the United States. As technology advances, the ability to create and publish documents will become easier and faster, thus influencing more businesses to produce printed materials. Desktop publishing specialists will be needed to satisfy typesetting, page layout, design, and editorial demands. With new equipment, commercial printing shops will be able to shorten the turnaround time on projects and in turn can increase business and accept more jobs. For instance, digital printing presses allow printing shops to print directly to the digital press rather than printing to a piece of film, and then printing from the film to the press. Digital printing presses eliminate an entire step and should appeal to companies who need jobs completed quickly.

According to a survey conducted by PIA in 1997, the printing industry is growing, which can be attributed partly to the growth experienced by the North American economy. The electronic prepress segment of the printing market enjoyed the most growth, with an average change from 1996 of 9.3 percent. Traditional prepress, on the other hand, suffered a decline of 5.7 percent. PIA's survey also indicates that printing firms have been experiencing difficulties finding new, qualified employees. This is a good sign for desktop publishing specialists with skills and experience.

QuarkXPress, Adobe PageMaker, Macromedia FreeHand, Adobe Illustrator, and Adobe Photoshop are some programs often used in desktop publishing. Specialists with experience in these and other software will be in demand.

For More Information

For career information, and information about scholarships and education, contact:

Association for Suppliers of Printing, Publishing, and Converting Technologies (NPES)
1899 Preston White Drive
Reston, VA 20191-4367
Tel: 703-264-7200
Email: npes@npes.org
Web: http://www.npes.org

For scholarship information, contact:

National Scholarship Trust Fund of the Graphic Arts
200 Deer Run Road
Sewickley, PA 15143-2600
Tel: 800-900-GATF
Email: info@gatf.org
Web: http://www.gatf.org

For career brochures and information about grants and scholarships, contact:

Society for Technical Communication
901 North Stuart Street, Suite 904
Arlington, VA 22203-1854
Tel: 703-522-4114
Web: http://www.stc-va.org

To obtain an issue of Desktop Publishers Journal, *a trade magazine for desktop publishers, contact:*

Desktop Publishers Journal
462 Boston Street
Topfield, MA 01983-1232
Tel: 978-887-7900
Web: http://www.dtpjournal.com

Independent Computer Consultants Association (ICCA)
11131 South Towne Square, Suite F
St. Louis, MO 63123
Tel: 800-774-4222
Web: http://www.icca.org

Editors

School Subjects
English
Journalism

Personal Interests
Communication/ideas
Helping/teaching

Work Environment
Primarily indoors
Primarily one location

Minimum Education Level
Bachelor's degree

Salary Range
$21,000 to $45,000 to $67,000+

Certification or Licensing
None available

Outlook
Faster than the average

Overview

Editors perform a wide range of functions, but their primary responsibility is to ensure that text provided by writers is suitable in content, format, and style for the intended audiences. Readers are an editor's first priority. Among the employers of editors are book publishers, magazines, newspapers, newsletters, corporations of all kinds, advertising agencies, radio stations, television stations, and Internet sites. No accurate figures for numbers of editors employed are available, but the U.S. Department of Labor has estimated that 286,000 writers and editors were employed in 1996.

History

The history of book editing is tied closely to the history of the book and bookmaking and the history of the printing process. The 15th century invention of the printing press by German goldsmith Johannes Gutenberg and of movable type in the West revolutionized the craft of bookmaking. Books could now be mass-produced. It also became more feasible to make changes to copy before a book was put into production. Printing had been invented hundreds of years earlier in Asia, but books did not proliferate there as quickly as they did in the West, which saw millions of copies in print by 1500.

In the early days of publishing, authors worked directly with the printer, and the printer was often the publisher and seller of the author's work. Eventually, however, booksellers began to work directly with the authors and eventually took over the role of publisher. The publisher then became the middleman between author and printer.

The publisher worked closely with the author and sometimes acted as the editor; the word editor, in fact, derives from the Latin word edere or editum and means supervising or directing the preparation of text. Eventually, specialists were hired to perform the editing function. These editors, who were also called advisors or literary advisors in the 19th century, became an integral part of the publishing business.

The editor, also called the sponsor in some houses, sought out the best authors, worked with them, and became their advocate in the publishing house. So important did some editors become that their very presence in a publishing house could determine the quality of author that might be published there. Some author-editor collaborations have become legendary. The field has grown through the 20th century, with computers greatly speeding up the process by which editors move copy to the printer.

The Job

Editors work for many kinds of publishers, publications, and corporations. Editors' titles vary widely, not only from one area of publishing to another but also within each area.

Although some editors write for the organizations that employ them, most editors work with material provided by writers. For this reason, one of the most important steps in the editing process is acquiring the work of writers. In the fields of book and journal publishing, that work is usually performed by acquisitions editors, who are often called acquiring editors. Acquisitions editors may either generate their own ideas or use ideas provided by their publishers or other staff members. If they begin with an idea, they look for writers who can create an effective book or article based on that idea. One benefit of that method is that such ideas are ones that the editors believe are likely to be commercially successful or intellectually successful or both. Often, however, editors use ideas that they receive from writers in the form of proposals.

In some cases, the *acquisitions editor* will receive a complete manuscript from an author instead of a proposal. Most of the time, however, the writer will submit a query letter that asks whether the editor is interested in a particular idea. If the editor believes that the idea is salable and suitable for the publishing house, the editor will discuss the idea further with the writer. Unless the writer is well known or is known and trusted by the editor, the editor usually asks the writer for a sample chapter or section. If the editor likes the sample chapter and believes that the author can complete an acceptable manuscript, the publishing house will enter into a contract with the writer. In some cases, the editor will prepare that contract; in others, the contract will be prepared by the publisher or someone else at the publishing house. The contract will specify when the manuscript is due, how much the author will be paid, how long the manuscript must be, and what will happen if the author cannot deliver a manuscript that the editor believes is suitable for publication, among other things.

After the contract has been signed, the writer will begin work. The acquisitions editor must keep track of the author's progress. Publishing budgets must be prepared in advance so that vendors can be paid and books can be advertised, so it is important that the manuscript be delivered by the due date. Some authors work well on their own and complete their work efficiently and effectively. In many cases, however, authors have problems. They may need advice from the editor regarding content, style, or organization of information. Often, the editor will want to see parts of the manuscript as they are completed. That way, any problems in the writer's work can be identified and solved as soon as possible.

Some typical problems are statements the writer makes that may leave the publisher open to charges of libel or plagiarism. If this problem arises, the editor will require the writer to revise the manuscript. If the writer uses materials that were created by other people (such as long quotations, tables, or artwork), it may be necessary to request permission to use those materials. If permission is required but is not given, the materials cannot be used. It is usually the author's job to obtain permission, but sometimes that task is performed by the editor. In any case, the editor must make sure that necessary permissions are obtained. When an acceptable manuscript has been delivered, the acquisition editor's job is usually complete.

Some publishing houses have editors who specialize in working with authors. These *developmental editors* do not acquire manuscripts. Instead, they make sure the author stays on schedule and does a good job of organizing material and writing.

Once an acceptable manuscript has been delivered to the publishing house, it is turned over to *a copy editor.* This editor's job is to read the manuscript carefully and make sure that it is sufficiently well written, factually correct (sometimes this job is done by a researcher or fact checker), grammatically correct, and appropriate in tone and style for its intended readers. If a book is not well written, it is not likely to be well received by readers. If it is not factually correct, it will not be taken seriously by those who spot its errors. If it is not grammatically correct, it will not be understood. If it is not appropriate for its audience, it will be utterly useless. Any errors or problems in a printed piece reflect badly not only on the author but also on the publishing house.

The copy editor must be an expert in the English language, have a keen eye for detail, and know how to identify problems. The editor will simply correct some kinds of errors, but in some cases-especially when the piece deals with specialized material-the editor may need to ask, or query, the author about certain points. An editor must never change something that he or she does not understand, since one of the worst errors an editor can make is to change something that is correct to something that is incorrect.

After the manuscript has been edited by the copy editor, it may be (but is not always) sent to the author for review. When the editor and author have agreed on the final copy, the editor or another specialist will use various kinds of coding to mark the manuscript for typesetting. The codes, which usually correlate to information provided by a graphic designer, tell the typesetter which typefaces to use, how large to make the type, what the layout of the finished pages will look like, and where illustrations or other visual materials will be placed on the pages, among other things.

After the manuscript has been typeset and turned into galley proofs, or typeset copy that has not been divided into pages, the galleys are usually sent to the author to be checked. If the author finds errors or requests that changes be made, the copy editor or the production editor will oversee the process, determining which changes will be made.

Managing the editorial staff is the job of the *managing editor,* who draws up budgets for projects, oversees schedules, assigns projects to other editors, and ensures that the editorial staff is working efficiently. The managing editor's boss is the *editor-in-chief, editorial director,* or *executive editor.* This editor works closely with the publisher, determining the kinds of materials the house will publish and ensuring that the editorial staff carries out the wishes of the publisher. The editor-in-chief and managing editor also work closely with the heads of other departments, such as marketing, sales, and production.

The basic functions performed by magazine and newspaper editors are much like those performed by book editors, but a significant amount of the writing that appears in magazines and newspapers, or periodicals, is done by staff writers. Periodicals often use editors who specialize in specific areas, such as *city editors,* who oversee the work of reporters who specialize in local news, and department editors. *Department editors* specialize in areas such as business, fashion, sports, and features, to name only a few. These departments are determined by the interests of the audience that the periodical intends to reach. Like book houses, periodicals use copy editors, researchers, and fact checkers, but at small periodicals, one or a few editors may be responsible for tasks that would be performed by many people at a larger publication.

Requirements

High School

Editors must be expert communicators, so you should excel in English if you wish to be an editor. You must learn to write extremely well, since you will be correcting and even rewriting the work of others. If elective classes in writing are available in your school, take them. Study journalism and take communications courses. Work as a writer or editor for the school paper. Take a photography class. Since virtually all editors use computers, take computer courses. You absolutely must learn to type. If you cannot type accurately and rapidly, you will be at an extreme disadvantage. Don't forget, however, that a successful editor must have a wide range of knowledge. The more you know about many areas, the more likely you will be to do well as an editor. Don't hesitate to explore areas that you find interesting. Do everything you can to satisfy your intellectual curiosity. As far as most editors are concerned, there is no useless information.

Postsecondary Training

An editor must have a bachelor's degree, and advanced degrees are highly recommended for book editors and magazine editors. Most editors have degrees in English or journalism, but it is not unheard of for editors to major in other liberal arts. If you know that you want to specialize in a field such as scientific editing, you may wish to major in the area of science of your choice while minoring in English, writing, or journalism. There are many opportunities for editors in technical fields, since most of those who go into editing are interested primarily in the liberal arts. Many colleges offer courses in book editing, magazine design, general editing, and writing. Some colleges, such as the University of Chicago and Stanford University, offer programs in publishing, and many magazines and newspapers offer internships to students. Take advantage of these opportunities. It is extremely important that you gain some practical experience while you are in school. Work on the school paper or find a part-time job with a newspaper or magazine. Don't hesitate to work for a publication in a noneditorial position. The more you know about the publishing business, the better off you will be.

Other Requirements

Good editors are fanatics. Their passion for good writing comes close to the point of obsession. They are analytical people who know how to think clearly and communicate what they are thinking. They read widely. They not only recognize good English when they see it but also know what makes it good. If they read something they don't understand, they analyze it until they do understand it. If they see a word they don't know, they look it up. When they are curious about something, they take action and research the subject. They are not satisfied with not knowing things.

You must be detail oriented to succeed as an editor. You must also be patient, since you may have to spend hours turning a few pages of near-gibberish into powerful, elegant English. If you are the kind of person who can't sit still, you probably will not succeed as an editor. To be a good editor, you must be a self-starter who is not afraid to make decisions. You must be good not only at identifying problems but also at solving them, so you must be creative. If you are both creative and a perfectionist, editing may be the line of work for you.

Exploring

One of the best ways to explore the field of editing is to work on a school newspaper or other publication. The experience you gain will definitely be helpful, even if your duties are not strictly editorial. Being involved in writing, reporting, typesetting, proofreading, printing, or any other task related to publishing will help you to understand editing and how it relates to the entire field of publishing.

If you cannot work for the school paper, try to land a part-time job on a local newspaper or newsletter. If that doesn't work, you might want to publish your own newsletter. There is nothing like trying to put together a small publication to make you understand how publishing works. You may try combining another interest with your interest in editing. For example, if you are interested in environmental issues, you might want to start a newsletter that deals with environmental problems and solutions in your community. Use your imagination.

Another useful project is keeping a journal. In fact, any writing project will be helpful, since editing and writing are inextricably linked. Write something every day. Try to rework your writing until it is as good as you can make it. Write about anything that you find interesting. Write letters to the editor, short stories, poetry, essays—anything you like.

Employers

One of the best things about the field of editing is that there are many kinds of opportunities for editors. The most obvious employers for editors are book publishers, magazines, and newspapers. There are many varieties of all three of these types of publishers. There are small and large publishers, general and specialized publishers, local and national publishers. If you have a strong interest in a particular field, you will undoubtedly find various publishers that specialize in it.

Another excellent source of employment is business. Almost all businesses of any size need writers and editors on a full-time or part-time basis. Corporations often publish newsletters for their employees or produce publications that talk about how they do business. Large companies produce annual reports that must be written and edited. In addition, advertising is a major source of work for editors, proofreaders, and writers. Advertising agencies use editors, proofreaders, and quality-control people, as do typesetting and printing companies (in many cases, proofreaders edit as well as proofread). Keep in mind that somebody has to work on all the printed material you see every day, from books and magazines to menus and matchbooks.

Starting Out

There is tremendous competition for editorial jobs, so it is important for a beginner who wishes to break into the business to be as well prepared as possible. College students who have gained experience as interns, have worked for publications during the summers, or have attended special programs in publishing will be at an advantage. In addition, applicants for any editorial position must be extremely careful when preparing cover letters and resumes. Even a single error in spelling or usage will disqualify an applicant. Applicants for editorial or proofreading positions must also expect to take and pass tests that are designed to determine their language skills.

Many editors enter the field as editorial assistants or proofreaders. Some editorial assistants perform only clerical tasks, whereas others may also proofread or perform basic editorial tasks. Typically, an editorial assistant who performs well will be given the opportunity to take on more and more editorial duties as time passes. Proofreaders have the advantage of being able to look at the work of editors, so they can learn while they do their own work.

Good sources of information about job openings are school placement offices, classified ads in newspapers and trade journals, specialized publications such as *Publishers Weekly* (a good source of jobs in book publishing), and Internet sites. One way to proceed is to identify local publishers through the Yellow Pages. Many publishers have Web sites that list job openings, and large publishers often have telephone job lines that serve the same purpose.

Advancement

In book houses, employees who start as editorial assistants or proofreaders and show promise generally become copy editors. After gaining skill in that position, they may be given a wider range of duties while retaining the same title. The next step may be a position as a senior copy editor, which involves overseeing the work of junior copy editors, or as a project editor. The project editor performs a wide variety of tasks, including copyediting, coordinating the work of in-house and freelance copy editors, and managing the schedule of a particular project. From this position, an editor may move up to become first assistant editor, then managing editor, then editor-in-chief. These positions involve more management and decision making than is usually found in the positions described previously. The editor-in-chief works with the publisher to ensure that a suitable editorial policy is being followed, while the managing editor is responsible for all aspects of the editorial department. The assistant editor provides support to the managing editor.

Newspaper editors generally begin working on the copy desk, where they progress from less significant stories and projects to major news and feature stories. A common route to advancement is for copy editors to be promoted to a particular department, where they may move up the ranks to management positions. An editor who has achieved success in a department may become a city editor, who is responsible for news, or a managing editor, who runs the entire editorial operation of a newspaper.

Magazine editors advance in much the same way that book editors do. After they become copy editors, they work their way up to become senior editors, managing editors, and editors-in-chief. In many cases, magazine editors advance by moving from a position on one magazine to the same position with a larger or more prestigious magazine. Such moves often bring significant increases in both pay and status.

Earnings

Although a small percentage of editors are paid extremely well, the average editor is not well paid. Competition for editing jobs is fierce, and there is no shortage of people who wish to enter the field. For that reason, companies that employ editors generally pay relatively low wages.

In July of 1998, *Publishers Weekly*, an important source of information about the book business, published a salary survey that stated that entry-level positions generally pay between $25,000 and $45,000, more advanced positions pay between $52,000 and $53,800, and supervisory positions pay between $45,000 and $88,700. It is worth noting that the vast majority of beginning editors will be paid salaries that are in line with the lower end of the range quoted above. Beginning salaries in the teens and low twenties are still common in many areas. The salaries of magazine editors are roughly comparable to those of book editors.

According to the Dow Jones Newspaper Fund, the average beginning salary for an editorial assistant was $21,000 in 1996, and it is reasonable to assume that that figure has not increased significantly. The Newspaper Guild has estimated that editors with at least five years of experience averaged more than $30,000 in 1996, while senior editors at large papers made more than $67,000 per year. Salaries for book and magazine editors were similar to those of newspaper editors.

Technical editors usually make more money than newspaper, magazine, or book editors. In 1996, the median salary for technical writers was $44,000, according to the Technical Communicators Salary Survey, and it is likely that the figure for technical editors was similar. The U.S. Department of Labor's *Occupational Outlook Handbook* has estimated that the average salary earned in 1996 by technical editors employed by the federal government was $47,000, while that earned by government-employed nontechnical editors was $46,590.

Work Environment

The environments in which editors work vary widely. For the most part, publishers of all kinds realize that a quiet atmosphere is conducive to work that requires tremendous concentration. It takes an unusual ability to focus in a noisy place. Most editors work in private offices or cubicles. Book editors often work in quieter surroundings than do newspaper editors or quality-control people in advertising agencies, who sometimes work in rather loud and hectic situations.

Even in relatively quiet surroundings, however, editors often have many distractions. A project editor who is trying to do some copyediting or review the editing of others may, for example, have to deal with phone calls from authors, questions from junior editors, meetings with members of the editorial and production staff, and questions from freelancers, among many other distractions. In many cases, editors have computers that are exclusively for their own use, but in others, editors must share computers that are located in a common area.

Deadlines are an important issue for virtually all editors. Newspaper and magazine editors work in a much more pressurized atmosphere than book editors because they face daily or weekly deadlines, whereas book production usually takes place over several months.

In almost all cases, editors must work long hours during certain phases of the editing process. Some newspaper editors start work at 5 AM, others work until 11 PM or even through the night. Feature editors, columnists, and editorial page editors usually can schedule their day in a more regular fashion, as can editors who work on weekly newspapers. Editors working on hard news, however, may receive an assignment that must be completed, even if work extends well into the next shift.

Outlook

According to the *Occupational Outlook Handbook,* employment of editors will increase faster than the average through 2006. At the same time, however, competition for those jobs will remain intense, since so many people want to enter the field. Book publishing will remain particularly competitive, since many people still view the field in a romantic light. Much of the expansion in publishing is expected to occur in small newspapers, radio stations, and television stations. In these organizations, pay is low even by the standards of the publishing business.

One of the major trends in publishing is specialization. More and more publishing ventures are targeting relatively narrow markets, which means that there are more opportunities for editors to combine their work and their personal interests. It is also true, however, that many of these specialty publications do not survive for long.

A fairly large number of positions—both full time and freelance—become available when experienced editors leave the business for other fields. Many editors make this decision because they find that they can make more money in other businesses than they can as editors.

For More Information

The following organization is an excellent source of information about careers in copyediting. The ACES organizes educational seminars and maintains lists of internships.

American Copy Editors Society
11690B Sunrise Valley Drive
Reston, VA 20191-1409
Tel: 703-453-1122
Email: asne@asne.org
Web: http://www.copydesk.org

The AAP is an organization of book publishers. Its extensive Web site is a good place to begin learning about the book business.

Association of American Publishers
71 Fifth Avenue
New York, NY 10010-2368
Tel: 212-255-0200
Email: aphillips@publishers.org
Web: http://www.publishers.org

The Fund provides information about internships and about the newspaper business in general.

Dow Jones Newspaper Fund
PO Box 300
Princeton, NJ 08543-0300
Tel: 609-452-2820
Email: newsfund@wsj.dowjones.com
Web: http://www.dowjones.com

The EFA is an organization for freelance editors. Members receive a newsletter and a free listing in their directory.

Editorial Freelancers Association
71 West 23rd Street, Suite 1504
New York, NY 10010
Tel: 212-929-5400
Web: http://www.the-efa.org

The MPA is a good source of information about internships.
Magazine Publishers of America
919 Third Avenue, 22nd Floor
New York, NY 10022
Tel: 212-872-3700
Web: http://www.magazine.org

The Slot is a Web site founded and maintained by Bill Walsh, financial copy desk chief at The Washington Post. *One of its most significant features is* The Curmudgeon's Stylebook, *a user-friendly guide to style and usage.*

The Slot
Web: http://www.theslot.com

Foreign Correspondents

	School Subjects
English Foreign language	
	Personal Skills
Communication/ideas Helping/teaching	
	Work Environment
Indoors and outdoors Primarily multiple locations	
	Minimum Education Level
Bachelor's degree	
	Salary Range
$50,000 to $75,000 to $100,000	
	Certification or Licensing
None available	
	Outlook
Little change or more slowly than the average	

Overview

Foreign correspondents report on news from countries outside of where their newspapers, radio or television networks, or wire services are located. Foreign correspondents sometimes work for a particular newspaper, but since today's media are more interested in local and national news, they usually rely on reports from news wire services to handle international news coverage rather than dispatching their own reporters to the scene. Only the biggest newspapers and television networks employ foreign correspondents. These reporters are usually stationed in a particular city and cover a wide territory.

History

James Gordon Bennett, Sr. (1795-1872), a prominent United States journalist and publisher of the *New York Herald*, was responsible for many firsts in the newspaper industry. He was the first publisher to sell papers through newsboys, the first to use illustrations for news stories, the first to publish stock-market prices and daily financial articles, and he was the first to employ European correspondents. Bennett's son, James Gordon Bennett, Jr. (1841-1918), carried on the family business and in 1871 sent Henry M. Stanley to central Africa to find Dr. David Livingstone.

In the early days, even magazines employed foreign correspondents. Famous American poet Ezra Pound, for example, reported from London for *Poetry* and *The Little Review.*

The inventions of the telegraph, telephone, typewriter, portable typewriter, and the portable laptop computer all have contributed to the field of foreign correspondence.

The Job

The foreign correspondent is stationed in a foreign country where his or her job is to report on the news there. Foreign news can range from the violent (wars, coups, and refugee situations) to the calm (cultural events and financial issues). Although a domestic correspondent is responsible for covering specific areas of the news like politics, health, sports, consumer affairs, business, or religion, foreign correspondents are responsible for all of these areas in the country where they are stationed. A China-based correspondent, for example, could spend a day covering the new trade policy between the United States and China, and the next day report on the religious persecution of Christians by the Chinese government.

A foreign correspondent often is responsible for more than one country. Depending on where he or she is stationed, the foreign correspondent might have to act as a one-person band in gathering and preparing stories.

"There are times when the phone rings at five in the morning and you're told to go to Pakistan," said Michael Lev, Tokyo Bureau Chief for the *Chicago Tribune.* "You must keep your wits about you and figure out what to do next."

For the most part, Lev decides on his own story ideas, choosing which ones interest him the most out of a myriad of possibilities. But foreign correspondents alone are responsible for getting the story done, and unlike reporters back home, they have little or no support staff to help them. Broadcast foreign correspondents, for example, after filming scenes may have to do their own audio editing. And just like other news reporters, foreign correspondents work under the pressure of deadlines. In addition, they often are thrown into unfamiliar situations in strange places.

Part of the importance of a foreign correspondent's job is keeping readers or viewers aware of the various cultures and practices held by the rest of the world. Lev says he tries to focus on similarities and differences between the Asian countries he covers and the United States. "If you don't understand another culture, you are more likely to come into conflict with it," he says.

Foreign correspondents are drawn to conflicts of all kinds, especially war. They may choose to go to the front of a battle to get an accurate picture of what's happening. Or they may be able to get the story from a safer position. Sometimes they face weapons trained directly on them.

Much of a foreign correspondent's time is spent doing research, investigating leads, setting up appointments, making travel arrangements, making on-site observations, and interviewing local people or those involved in the situation. The foreign correspondent often must be experienced in taking photographs or shooting video.

Living conditions can be rough or primitive, sometimes with no running water. The job can prove isolating.

After correspondents have interviewed sources and noted observations about an event or filmed it, they put their stories together, writing on computers and using modern technology like the Internet, email, satellite telephones, and fax machines to finish the job and transmit the story to their newspaper, broadcast station, or wire service. Many times, correspondents work out of hotel rooms.

Requirements

High School

In addition to English and creative writing needed for a career in journalism, you should study languages, social studies, political science, history, and geography. Initial experience may be gained by working on your school newspaper or yearbook, or taking advantage of study-abroad programs.

Postsecondary Training

In college, obtaining a journalism major is helpful but may not be crucial to obtaining a job as a foreign correspondent. Classes, or even a major, in political science or literature could be beneficial. Economics and foreign languages also help.

Other Requirements

To be a foreign correspondent, in addition to a definite love of adventure, you need curiosity about how other people live, diplomacy when interviewing people, courage to sometimes confront people on uncomfortable topics, ability to communicate well, and the discipline to sometimes act as your own boss. You also need to be strong enough to hold up under pressure yet flexible enough to adapt to other cultures.

Employers

Foreign correspondents work for news wire services, such as the Associated Press, Reuters, and Agence-France Press, major metropolitan newspapers, news magazines, and television and radio networks. These media are located in the nation's largest cities and in the case of Reuters and Agence-France Press, in Europe.

Starting Out

College graduates have a couple of paths to choose between to become a foreign correspondent. They can decide to experience what being a foreign correspondent is like immediately by going to a country, perhaps one whose language is familiar to them, and freelancing or working as a stringer. That means writing stories and offering them to anyone who will buy them. This method can be hard to accomplish financially in the short run but can pay off substantially in the long run.

This is the route Judith Matloff, foreign correspondent for the *Christian Science Monitor,* took. She started out freelancing in Mexico for English-speaking newspapers, publications, and wire services. Nine months after selling her first freelance article, the wire service Reuters offered her a job and her career took off.

Another path is to take the traditional route of a journalist and try to get hired upon graduation at any newspaper, radio station, or television station you can. It helps in this regard to have worked at a summer internship during your college years. Recent college graduates generally get hired at small newspapers or media stations, although a few major metropolitan dailies will employ top graduates for a year with no guarantee of them being kept on afterward. After building experience at a small paper or station, a reporter can try to find work at progressively bigger ones. Reporters who find employment at a major metropolitan daily that uses foreign correspondents can work their way through the ranks to become one. This is the path Lev took and he became a foreign correspondent when he was in his early 30s. He suggests that working for a wire service may allow a reporter to get abroad faster, but he thinks more freedom can be found working for a newspaper.

Advancement

Foreign correspondents can advance to other locations that are more appealing to them or that offer a bigger challenge. Or they can return home to become columnists, editorial writers, editors, or network news directors.

Earnings

Salaries vary greatly depending on the publication, network, or station, and the cost of living and tax structure in various places around the world where foreign correspondents work. Generally, salaries range from $50,000 to an average of about $75,000 to a peak of $100,000 or more. Some media will pay for living expenses, such as the costs of a home, school for the reporter's children, and a car.

Outlook

Although employment at newspapers, radio stations, and television stations in general is expected to continue to decline, the number of foreign correspondent jobs has leveled off. The employment outlook is expected to remain relatively stable, or even increase should a major conflict or war occur.

Factors that keep the number of foreign correspondents low are the high cost of maintaining a foreign news bureau and the relative lack of interest Americans show in world news. Despite these factors, the number of correspondents is not expected to decrease. There are simply too few as it is; decreasing the number could put the job in danger of disappearing, which most journalists believe is not an option. For now and the near future, you can expect most job openings to arise from the need to replace those correspondents who leave the job.

For More Information

The ASJA provides information on careers in newspaper reporting, as well as information on education and financial aid.

American Society of Journalists and Authors
1501 Broadway, Suite 302
New York, NY 10036
Tel: 212-997-0947
Email: 75227.1650@compuserve.com
Web: http://www.asja.org/cw950615.htm

The AEJMC provides general educational information on all areas of journalism (newspapers, magazines, television, and radio).

Association for Education in Journalism and Mass Communication
Lew Conte College, Room 121
Columbia, SC 29208-0251
Tel: 803-777-2005
Web: http://www.rwonline.com/orgnztns/olist/org-aejmc.html

The NAB has information on jobs, scholarships, internships, college programs, and other resources. It offers Careers in Radio *($4) and* Careers in Television *($4), which describe the key jobs, educational requirements, and job-related experience required.*

National Association of Broadcasters
1771 N Street, NW
Washington, DC 20036
Tel: 202-429-5300
Email: jearnhar@nab.org
Web: http://www.nab.org

The SPJ has student chapters all over the United States. Among its many services to students, it offers information on scholarships and internships.

Society of Professional Journalists
16 South Jackson
Greencastle, IN 46135-0077
Email: spj@link2000.net
Web: http://www.spj.org

Grant Coordinators and Writers

School Subjects
Business
English

Personal Skills
Communication/ideas
Leadership/management

Work Environment
Primarily indoors
Primarily one location

Minimum Education Level
Bachelor's degree

Salary Range
$18,000 to $44,000 to $69,000

Certification or Licensing
None available

Outlook
Little change or more slowly than the average

Overview

Grant coordinators are responsible for managing all grant-funded programs for nonprofit organizations. *Grant writers* handle the actual creation and preparation of proposals to potential funders. In smaller organizations, both jobs may be handled by the same person. Both grant coordinators and grant writers may work for schools, local governments, social service agencies, and other organizations to oversee all aspects of grant funding. The National Society for Fund-Raising Executives reports that it has 17,000 members employed at a variety of nonprofit organizations, including those in the arts, social service, health care, and educational fields, as well as at private consulting firms around the country.

History

The first recorded government research grant was given to the inventor Samuel Morse in 1842. In the United States, the amount of grants funding has grown consistently and dramatically since that time. More private foundations began bestowing grants when it became clear how much help they could provide to all types of nonprofit groups. Government agencies have increased grants funding, especially in the sciences, recognizing that these grants help U.S. scientists and inventors stay on the cutting edge of new technology.

It is only in the last few decades that the positions of grant coordinator and grant writer have come into being. Organizing and writing grant proposals was usually assigned to various employees (who had other job duties) in each nonprofit agency. Now more and more agencies are recognizing the value of having separate grant coordinators and writers who work solely on grants for the agency.

The Job

The number of grants awarded each year in the United States is very large, and so is the competition among grants seekers; hundreds of institutions may apply for the same grant. Furthermore, organizations that award grants have very specific rules and requirements that must be satisfied for a proposal even to be considered.

Grant coordinators must be familiar with all applicable funding organizations and their requirements. They often make the difference in securing the grant for their organizations. Grant coordinators plan and organize all grant-funded programs for their agency or organization. Most foundations and grant-offering agencies publish information regarding their grants. Grant coordinators conduct extensive research on these organizations by receiving publications and contacting officials at the foundations.

To determine which grants the organization should apply for, coordinators work with other officers in their own agency. Grant coordinators participate in many of the planning stages for the agency. For instance, they may sit in on meetings in which budgets are planned and financial officials determine operating budgets, anticipate income, and forecast expenditures. Employees of the nonprofit organization may suggest programs, equipment, or materials that they would like to have funded by a grant, and the grant coordinator determines the best source of funding for such a program.

Often grants funding fills the gap between the operating expenses and other funding sources (such as individual donations) for a nonprofit organization. Before applying for a grant, a grant coordinator maps out a proposal for how the funding would be used. Often these proposals are long and complex. Other employees may help the grant coordinator write up a proposal justifying the need for the proposed program or equipment.

Some nonprofit organizations are fortunate enough to have one or more employees whose primary function is grant writing. In these cases the grant coordinator does not write the grant proposal. The grant writer creates the proposal document, developing its vocabulary and overall structure. Working with the staff whose programming requires funding, the grant writer devises a strategy, translating the program to make it relevant to the funder's interests. Also in the proposal, the grant writer must communicate both the short-term and long-term goals of the organization so that they are understandable to an outsider. The grant writer also may be responsible for assembling the supporting documents that accompany the proposal: the organization's budget, board of directors, history, mission, and executive biographies. The grant writer must create different proposals for different kinds of funding—for example, general operating support for the organization overall vs. funding for a specific program or project. Additionally, if a grant is received, the grant writer often has to prepare a final report required by many funders.

When an organization does not have a separate grant writer on staff, the writer may be a financial officer in the organization, a teacher in the school, or an employee in charge of a particular project. Here the grant coordinator works closely with the writer to help focus the proposal so that the funding agency will want to bestow the grant.

The proposal usually passes through many hands before being sent to foundations or grant-offering government agencies. Most nonprofit organizations have fiscal officers or other executives who first must approve the proposal. With their approval, the grant coordinator or writer prepares the grant proposal using the format required by the funding agency. The proposal then is submitted to the foundation or funding agency. It is the responsibility of the grant coordinator or writer to follow up on the application and meet with agency or foundation representatives if necessary.

Once the nonprofit agency receives its grant, the coordinator makes sure to meet all of the requirements of the granting organization. For example, if the grant covers the purchase of equipment, the coordinator confirms receipt of the correct equipment and completion of the follow-up reports sent to the foundation or agency. In some instances, the grant coordinator hires an outside agency to monitor the implementation of a grant-funded program. The outside agency then may submit its periodic monitoring reports both to the funding agency and to the grant coordinator.

A large part of the grant coordinator's work involves maintenance of files and overseeing paperwork, which is usually done on computer. A thorough grant coordinator must keep the literature published by funding agencies for reference and file copies of all applications and proposals.

Grant coordinators are essentially project managers. They must understand the overall work of their organization while focusing on finding and obtaining the best grants. They see to it that their organization presents itself to funding agencies in the best possible way.

Requirements

High School

High school students who are considering careers as grant coordinators or writers should take courses in English, journalism, and creative writing, to develop their written communication skills. Courses in history and the humanities in general also are useful as background reference, and a solid background in mathematics will help individuals feel comfortable dealing with budgets and other financial documents.

Postsecondary Training

Grant coordinators and writers almost always have bachelor's degrees. The degree can be a bachelor of arts, bachelor of science, or an equivalent degree from a four-year college or university. Grant coordinators and writers can have any of several kinds of educational backgrounds. Some study liberal arts, some have business degrees, and some have studied in management training programs. Common to all grant officers, regardless of their educational background, is the ability to communicate clearly and effectively in writing. Much paperwork is involved in applying for a grant; the funding agency's instructions must be followed to the letter, and the proposal must state the institution's goals and objectives in a clear and persuasive way.

Certification or Licensing

There is no licensing requirement or specific test that grant coordinators or writers must pass. While not required, the National Society of Fund-Raising Executives offers a Certification for Fund-Raising Executives Program and an Advanced Certification for Fund-Raising Executives Program.

Other Requirements

Most grant coordinators learn their work on the job. Experience in the workplace helps the coordinator locate the best sources of grants funding and learn the best ways to pursue those sources and implement the funding program. For example, often a foundation's ideals may match the intent of the grant coordinator's agency, which can result in an agency developing an ongoing relationship with a foundation. The grant coordinator learns about these connections in the day-to-day work.

Grant coordinators must have good administrative skills and be detail-oriented. Good communication skills are essential. They work with a wide range of people and must express themselves easily. Coordinators direct and supervise others, so they must be comfortable in management situations. They should be able to influence and persuade others, including their associates and foundation employees. The more grant coordinators and writers understand about the operations of the foundations that they will be applying to, the more successful they will be in writing the grant proposals and securing the requested funding. Grant coordinators and writers must also work well under pressure. There are deadlines to meet, and the responsibility for meeting those deadlines falls squarely on their shoulders. The financial pressure on an organization that does not receive an expected grant can be enormous, and the grant coordinator may bear the responsibility for the loss.

Exploring

Developing skills in research and expository writing is a good way to prepare for the job of grant coordinator or grant writer while still in high school. Volunteering for nonprofit organizations is a good way to find out about a grant coordinator's work firsthand. Students may contact local churches or synagogues, charities, health organizations, or social service agencies. In nonprofit organizations that have grant coordinators, the ideal internship or volunteer experience involves assisting with a grant application project. Sometimes schools have their own grant application projects several times annually. Students can get an understanding of all of the work involved by seeing the application project or proposal through from start to finish.

Several organizations sponsor intensive workshops on grant coordination and fund-raising. The Grantsmanship Center in Los Angeles conducts seminars and workshops in cities across the United States more than 200 times a year. They help grant coordinators and writers with proposal writing and other aspects of their jobs. Their newsletter, *Whole Nonprofit Catalog: A Compendium of Sources and Resources for Managers and Staff of Nonprofit Organizations*, is published quarterly, and reprints are available. Students who are interested in the field may want to obtain a few reprints of this newsletter. The Grantsmanship Center also maintains a reference library. The National Network of Grantmakers also runs seminars and offers publications.

Many fund-raising organizations also have helpful publications for the potential grant coordinator. An annual almanac, *Giving USA*, is published by the American Association of Fund-Raising Counsel.

Some colleges and universities offer courses in fund-raising. These may even include lectures or seminars on the grant application process. Many colleges also offer courses in arts management or in nonprofit work that would help potential grant coordinators and writers understand the type of work required in this occupation.

Employers

Grant writers and coordinators work for nonprofit organizations and agencies, such as social service agencies, arts organizations, museums, educational institutions, and research foundations.

Starting Out

After receiving a bachelor's degree, people interested in writing or coordinating grant proposals apply for jobs at nonprofit organizations. Most of the time they are hired to do other work at the organization first. Prospective grant coordinators and writers must learn how the organization operates and understand its goals before beginning to work with grants. Management training programs are helpful for potential grant coordinators, as are courses in technical writing, psychology, sociology, and statistical methods.

Advancement

Since grant coordinators almost always begin their careers in other work, they advance into grant positions by showing an understanding of the organization's goals. Once the organization moves a person into a grant position, advancement comes with successful work on grant proposals and obtaining the necessary funding. If the grant coordinator and writer positions are separate, usually grant writers advance to grant coordinators, having gained expertise and familiarity with the funding community. But because nonprofit organizations often employ only one person responsible for grant writing and coordination, a grant administrator advances by moving into a position with a larger nonprofit organization that requires higher-level skills.

Earnings

Grant coordinators earn comparable salaries to upper-level administrative personnel. Starting grant coordinators may earn between $18,000 and $25,000 per year. Some organizations may pay as much as $44,000 per year to a grant coordinator or fund-raiser who has been with the organization in a different position. Experienced grant coordinators who have proven success at obtaining and coordinating grants can earn $69,000, according to the National Association of Colleges and Employers.

Grant writers, if they hold separate positions, usually are paid less than grant coordinators. According to a fall 1996 salary survey of nonprofit organizations by Cordom Associates in Washington, DC, as reported in *National Business Employment Weekly,* the median salary for a staff writer (which includes grant writers) is $41,300, down half a percentage point from 1995.

Benefits for grant coordinators and writers often are equivalent to other professional business positions, including paid vacation, group insurance plans, and paid sick days.

Work Environment

Grant coordinators work primarily in comfortable office environments. Some nonprofit agencies have cramped or inadequate facilities, while others may be quite luxurious. The grant coordinator usually works during regular office hours unless a deadline must be met. When grant coordinators approach the deadlines for submitting grant proposals, overtime work, including nights or weekends, may be required. Meetings with foundation representatives may take place outside the office or before or after regular hours. Benefits packages and vacation time vary widely from agency to agency, but most nonprofit organizations are flexible places to work. Grant coordinators are often most satisfied with their jobs when they believe in the goals of their own agency and know they are helping the agency do its work.

Outlook

The outlook for grant coordinators and writers is steady until the year 2006. However, hundreds of agencies are applying for the same grants, and the grant coordinator or writer can make the difference between the organization that gets the funding and the one that does not. A grant coordinator who has proven success in coordinating grants proposals and obtaining grants, as well as a grant writer who has written successful proposals, should be able to find work. Many people who work in nonprofit organizations believe that more grant coordinators and writers will be hired as more of these organizations realize that a professional grant administrator may help them get funding they have been missing. The grant coordinator's knowledge of how to choose the most appropriate sources of grant funding and implement funding programs is invaluable to nonprofit organizations.

For More Information

The following is a coalition of consulting firms working in the nonprofit sector.

American Association of Fund-Raising Counsels
25 West 43rd Street, Suite 1519
New York, NY 10036
Tel: 212-354-5799
Web: http://www.aafrc.org

The following organization provides assistance on proposal writing, offers 200 seminars annually, and publishes a quarterly newsletter.

The Grantsmanship Center
1125 West 6th Street, 5th Floor
Los Angeles, CA 90017
Tel: 213-482-9860
Email: marc@tgci.com
Web: http://www.tgci.com

This professional association is for individuals responsible for generating philanthropic support for nonprofits. It provides educational programs, a resource center, conference, and quarterly journal. It has 17,000 members and 149 chapters.

National Society of Fund-Raising Executives
1101 King Street, Suite 700
Alexandria, VA 22314-2967
Tel: 703-684-0410
Email: nsfre@nsfre.org
Web: http://www.nsfre.org

Greeting Card Designers and Writers

	School Subjects
Art	
English	
Computer science	

	Personal Skills
Artistic	
Communication/ideas	

	Work Environment
Primarily indoors	
Primarily one location	

	Minimum Education Level
High school diploma	

	Salary Range
$15/idea to $50/idea to $150/idea	

	Certification or Licensing
None available	

	Outlook
About as fast as the average	

Overview

Greeting card designers and writers either work freelance or as staff members of greeting card and gift manufacturers. Designers use artistic skills to create illustrated or photographic images for cards, posters, mugs, and other items generally sold in card shops; writers compose the expressions, poems, and jokes that accompany the images. The Greeting Card Association estimates that there are more than 1,500 large and small greeting card publishers in America.

History

The Valentine is considered by many to be the earliest form of greeting card. Up until the fifth century, Romans celebrated a fertility festival called Lupercalia every February 15. At the feast, women wrote love notes and dropped them in an urn; the men would pick a note from the urn, then seek the company of the woman who composed the note. But the mass-produced holiday cards we know today didn't really originate until the 1880s in England and America. With printing costs and postage rates low, the colorful, cheerful, and beautifully illustrated cards of the day quickly grew in popularity.

The Job

From statements of love to rude insults, the contemporary greeting card industry provides a note for practically every expression. Hallmark and American Greetings are the biggest names in the business, offering cards for many occasions; other card companies have carved out their own individual niches, like C-ya ("relationship closure cards" to send to ex-boyfriends, for-mer bosses, and anybody you don't ever want to see again) and Mixed Blessing (which sells "interfaith and multicultural holiday products" such as cards and products that combine symbols of Christmas and Hanukkah, including the book "Blintzes for Blitzen"). Though some of these companies use the talents of full-time staff writers and designers, others rely on free-lancers to submit ideas, images, and expressions. In addition to greeting card production, some companies buy words and images for email greetings, and for lines of products like mugs, posters, pillows, and balloons.

Bonnie Neubauer, a freelance writer in Pennsylvania, has tapped into the "business to business" greeting card niche. "They're tools to help sales peo-ple," Bonnie explains. "They help business people keep in touch." She sells her ideas to a small company called IntroKnocks, but many greeting card companies are getting into the business of business-to-business cards. Hallmark and Gibson, two of the biggest card manufacturers, now sell cards to brighten up the workplace. "So many people communicate through faxes, emails, voicemail," Bonnie says, "that when a card comes in a colored enve-lope, with a hand-written address, it gets attention." To spark ideas, Bonnie reads industry trade magazines, visits company Web sites, and looks over a book of stock photos. Once recognizing a business need, she comes up with a card to meet the need. "Some people only send out cartoons," she says about the business-to-business greeting card marketplace, "some people are more serious, and want only cards with sophisticated photographs."

Working from home offices, greeting card writers and designers come up with their ideas, then submit them to the companies for consideration. "Coming up with good card ideas," Bonnie says, "involves taking cliches, and combining them with a tad of humor." Artists and photographers submit reproductions of their work, rather than their originals, because some companies don't return unaccepted submissions or may lose the submissions in the review process. Artists submit prints, color xeroxes, duplicate transparencies, or floppy disks. Writers submit their ideas on index cards (one idea per index card).

Requirements

High School

Hone your writing and artistic skills in high school by taking English and art classes. Since many designers use computers to create their designs, computer science courses also will be helpful.

Postsecondary Training

College education is not necessary for freelancing as an artist and writer, though card companies looking to hire you for a full-time staff position may require a background in English, creative writing, graphic design, or commercial arts. Even if you only want to freelance, community college courses that instruct you in the use of computer design programs can help you to create professional-looking images for submission to companies.

Certification or Licensing

No certification program exists for greeting card writers/designers. But if you decide to print your own cards and sell them to stores and representatives, you may be required by your state to maintain a business license.

Other Requirements

"I'm extremely self-motivated," Bonnie says, in regard to making her home business a success, "and grossly optimistic." As for the writing itself, Bonnie emphasizes the importance of a sense of humor. "I love word-play," she says, "and I love marketing and promotions." Any writer and designer should also be patient, persistent, and capable of taking rejection.

Exploring

Try writing and designing your own greeting cards. There are many software programs that will help you create attractive cards, stationery, and newsletters. Ask your high school English teacher or counselor to set up an interview with a greeting card designer or freelance writer.

Employers

As a freelancer, you can work anywhere in the country, and submit your work through the mail. *Writer's Market,* a reference book published annually by Writer's Digest Books, includes a section listing the greeting card companies that accept submissions from freelance writers and artists. While some companies only buy a few ideas a year, others buy hundreds of ideas. Hallmark, by far the largest greeting card manufacturer, doesn't accept unsolicited ideas, but hires many creative people for full-time staff positions. Because of Hallmark's reputation as a great employer, competition for those positions is high.

Starting Out

Get to know the market by visiting local card shops; find out what's popular, and what kinds of cards each company sells. Visit the Web sites of the greeting card companies listed in *Writer's Market* and study their online catalogs. Most companies have very specific guidelines—one may publish only humorous cards, while another may only publish inspirational poems. Once you have a good sense of what companies might be interested in your work, write them or call them to find out their submission guidelines. Also, each spring, Hallmark holds an annual competition for their writing and editing internships.

Advancement

After you've submitted a lot of your work to many different companies, you'll begin to make connections with people in the business. These connections can be valuable, and may result in better pay (such as royalties and percentages) and exclusive contracts. As you get to know the business better, you may choose to produce and market your own line of cards. Sally Silagy, who owns Gardening Greetings, sells a Home-Based Greeting Card Kit, which details her own experiences with starting a business, and offers instruction into how to get started.

Earnings

Salaries vary widely among freelance greeting card writers/designers. Designers and artists can typically make more money for their work than writers. Some card designer/writers sell only a few ideas a year. Others make a great deal of money, working exclusively with a company, or by manufacturing and distributing their own lines of cards and products. Card companies typically pay freelancers fees for each idea they buy. Some companies may offer a royalty payment plan, including an initial advance. A small company may pay as little as $15 for an idea, while a larger company may pay $150 or more.

Work Environment

Both as a writer and as a designer, you'll be spending much of your time in your home office. Some of your time will be in front of the computer, designing images, or writing copy. Coming up with the initial ideas, however, may involve pampering yourself so that you can be at your most creative—many artists have certain routines to inspire them, such as listening to music, looking at photography and art books, or reading a novel.

Outlook

According to the Greeting Card Association (an organization representing card companies), the greeting card industry's retail sales have increased steadily from $2.1 billion in 1980, to over $7 billion in 1997. From designing animated email messages to greeting card CD-ROM programs, greeting card writers/designers will likely find more and more outlets for their work. Advances in Web technology should also aid the card designer who can post ideas and images, and invite companies to browse, download, and pay for the ideas online.

For More Information

For an application for Hallmark's internship program, write to:

Hallmark-CRWEB
Creative Writing Summer Intern Competition
Creative Staffing and Development, #444
2501 McGee
Kansas City, MO 64108
Web: http://www.hallmark.com

Visit your library or bookstore for a copy of the latest edition of Writer's Market, *or contact:*

Writer's Digest Books
1507 Dana Avenue
Cincinnati, OH 45207

For price and other information for Sally Silagy's Home-Based Greeting Card Kit, which details how to start your own greeting card business, contact:

Gardening Greetings
189a Paradise Circle
Woodland Park, CO 80863
Web: http://www.gardeninggreetings.com

Indexers

School Subjects	Computer science English
Personal Skills	Communication/ideas Helping/teaching
Work Environment	Primarily indoors Primarily one location
Minimum Education Level	Bachelor's degree
Salary Range	$20,000 to $30,000 to $70,000
Certification or Licensing	None available
Outlook	About as fast as the average

Overview

Indexers compile organized lists, called indexes, that help people locate information in a text or body of work. Indexes are like "road maps" that help users find desired information. Just as a map allows travelers to select the most direct route to a destination, indexes should provide users with a basis for selecting relevant information and screening out that which is unwanted.

History

The first known finding list was compiled by Callimachus, a Greek poet and scholar of the 3rd century BC, to provide a guide to the contents of the Alexandrian Library. Primitive alphabetical indexes began to appear in the 16th century AD. In 1614, the bishop of Petina, Antonio Zara, included an index in his *Anatomia ingeniorum etscientiarum (Anatomy of Talents and Sciences)*, and in 1677, Johann Jacob Hoffman added an index to his *Lexicon universale*. These early indexes were difficult to use because entries under each letter of the alphabet were not arranged alphabetically. Every term beginning with a "B" would appear somewhere under that letter, but subjects beginning "Ba" did not necessarily precede those beginning "Be."

In the 18th century, alphabetic indexing improved, as demonstrated in Denis Diderot's (1713-84) *Encyclopedie,* which is alphabetized consistently throughout. In the 19th century, indexers attempted to compile indexes that covered entire fields of knowledge. The *Reader's Guide to Periodic Literature,* published by H.W. Wilson Company of New York, is one of the best-known examples of an index that includes references to many publications.

The 20th century revolutionized the fields of indexing and information retrieval by introducing computer technology. There are now many computer programs designed to assist in the preparation of indexes. Some programs, in fact, have largely automated the mechanical aspects of indexing.

The Job

There are several types of common indexes. The most familiar is the back-of-book index. Back-of-book indexes contain references to information in only one volume. Most nonfiction, single-volume texts include this sort of index. Multivolume indexes contain references to information in more than one volume. The page references in a multivolume index must indicate clearly both the volume number and the page number of the cited information. Most encyclopedias include multivolume indexes. Magazines and newspapers also have indexes. These periodical indexes are published separately, at regular intervals throughout the year, and are extremely helpful to researchers.

A more recent development in indexing is the online index. Online indexes help users locate specific information from within a large database. Online indexes differ from a simple search function in that an indexer has created a translational thesaurus. When a user inputs a term that actually does not exist in the database, the online index will translate the term to a synonym that does exist so that the user may access the needed information.

Though their scope and purposes vary widely, all indexes have certain features in common. Every index must be organized according to a useful system. Most indexes are alphabetical, though in some specialized cases they may be chronological or numerical. The index to a history text, for instance, might be in chronological order. The two most commonly used alphabetical filing systems are the word-by-word arrangement, under which New York would precede Newark, and the letter-by-letter arrangement, under which New York would follow Newark.

All indexes must contain index terms, called headings, and page numbers or other locators. Most indexes also contain subheadings that help users narrow their search for information. Under the main heading "George Washington," for example, an indexer might use subheadings to separate references to the Revolutionary War from those to Washington's presidency. An index also may include cross-references to other pertinent headings or indicate the presence of illustrations, charts, and bibliographies.

Whether one creates an index on three-by-five index cards or with the help of a software program, the mental process is the same. The indexer first must read and understand the primary information in the text. Only then can the indexer begin to identify key terms and concepts. The second phase in compiling an index is called tracing—marking terms or concepts. Choosing appropriate headings is often the most challenging aspect of an indexer's job. Subjects must be indexed not only under the terms used in the text, but also under the terms that may occur to the reader. Since the indexer's first obligation is to help the reader find information, the best indexers ask themselves, "Where would the reader look?"

After tracing, the indexer begins to compile the headings and page references. Entries with many page citations must be divided further by subheadings. The final step in creating an index is editing. The indexer must view the index as a whole in order to polish the organization, delete trivial references, and add appropriate subheadings.

While indexers may organize information by key words or concepts, the most useful indexes usually combine both systems. Key word compilation is indiscriminate and is of limited usefulness to the reader. Key word lists include every instance of a term and usually fail to make connections between synonymous or related terms. Computer programs that promise automated indexing are actually capable only of compiling such key word concordances. In conceptual indexing, on the other hand, the indexer is not bound to standardized terminology, but recognizes synonymous or related information and disregards trivial references. Even the most sophisticated computer program is incapable of creating an adequate conceptual index.

Requirements

High School

Although there is no one educational path that best prepares students to become indexers, a high school diploma and a college degree are necessary. Classes in English and computers are essential, and classes in history and other social sciences will provide familiarity with a broad range of subjects that might be indexed.

Postsecondary Training

Since indexers must be well-read and knowledgeable about a wide range of academic disciplines, a liberal arts degree is highly recommended. Many indexers have one or more advanced degrees as well. Professional training is not required but can be extremely helpful. Though few educational institutions offer indexing courses, many offer relevant classes that may be useful to indexers, such as Information Storage and Retrieval, Introduction to Information Science, and Cataloging and Classification.

Today's indexers must be computer literate to be competitive. Manual preparation of indexes is a dying art due to the widespread availability of computer programs designed to automate the mechanics of indexing. This trend toward computer-assisted indexing will continue as more and more information is created and stored in electronic format. Tomorrow's indexers will often create online indexes for large databases rather than the familiar back-of-book variety. With the incredible proliferation of information in the late 20th century, information management has become an increasingly complex and competitive field. Those who would be indexers must be prepared to adapt rapidly as methods of storing and disseminating information continue to change and advance in the 21st century. With this in mind, aspiring indexers would do well to pursue degrees in library or information science.

Other Requirements

Indexing can be an extremely solitary profession. Indexers should enjoy intellectual challenges and have a passion for coherent structure. To be successful, indexers must also have great patience for detail.

Exploring

To explore the indexing profession, interested high school students should visit libraries to read and evaluate indexes of all kinds. Students also should read some basic books on the practice and theory of indexing, such as *Indexing Books: An Introduction* by Nancy Mulvany or *Indexing from A to Z* by Hans Wellisch. The American Society of Indexers publishes several helpful pamphlets on getting started in the indexing profession. Correspondence courses are available through the U.S. Department of Agriculture.

Employers

Traditionally, indexers have worked for publishers of books or periodicals. Publishers of encyclopedias, legal books, and newspapers usually employ a staff of indexers. They are full-time employees, or they earn a living by freelance indexing. Freelance indexers are self-employed workers who sell their indexing services. Publishers hire freelance indexers to work on specific books or projects.

Starting Out

Novice indexers can enter the field by becoming a junior member of an indexing team at a large publishing house. Beginners commonly work under the close supervision of a more experienced staff member. Freelance indexers begin by soliciting work—a time-consuming and difficult process. In order to gain experience and build client relationships, novice indexers must initially accept small jobs at relatively low pay rates.

Advancement

Junior indexers may advance to positions of greater seniority in two to three years. Eventually, an indexer can attain a supervisory position within an indexing department. Experienced freelance indexers may charge reasonably higher rates as their level of expertise increases.

Earnings

The average salary for a beginning indexer was $20,000 in 1996. More experienced indexers can earn $25,000 to $30,000 as they acquire more supervisory responsibilities and seniority. Freelance indexing has the potential to be more lucrative than in-house indexing, but offers less financial security. Freelance indexers must provide their own offices, equipment, and health insurance. In general, hourly rates more accurately reflect the indexer's efforts than per entry or per page rates because indexes which involve extensive conceptual work may have relatively few entries. Freelance indexers can earn from $20,000 to $70,000 annually, depending on their level of experience.

Work Environment

Full-time indexers usually work between 35 and 40 hours a week in typical office settings. Freelance indexers may work out of their homes or take temporary assignments in the offices of employers. The amount of pressure an indexer experiences varies greatly with the type of indexing. Those who compile indexes for newspapers must sift rapidly through great quantities of information and regularly work long hours. Encyclopedia indexers, on the other hand, may face deadlines only once a year. Freelance indexers have irregular schedules; a freelance indexer may work extremely long hours when completing several projects at once but have relatively little work the following week. In general, freelance indexing is more stressful than in-house work as freelancers must constantly plan out their own work schedules, send invoices, and keep business records, in addition to indexing.

Outlook

Publishers in the 21st century will tend toward computer-assisted indexing, making it necessary for indexers to be well versed in the use of computer programs. Computers are not likely to replace human indexers who have thought-processing abilities anytime soon, however; publishers of reference material, newspapers, and scholarly works will continue to value competent indexers. In addition, as information replaces manufacturing as the world's most valuable industry, new opportunities for indexers should become available.

For More Information

American Society of Indexers
PO Box 39366
Phoenix, AZ 85069-9366
Tel: 602-979-5514
Email: info@asindexing.org
Web: http://www.asindexing.org

Correspondence Study Program
Graduate School, USDA
A.G. Box 9911, Room 1112-South
Washington, DC 20250

Interpreters and Translators

School Subjects
English
Foreign language

Personal Skills
Communication/ideas
Following instructions

Work Environment
Primarily indoors
Primarily multiple locations

Minimum Education Level
Bachelor's degree

Salary Range
$12,000 to $31,800 to $75,000

Certification or Licensing
Recommended

Outlook
About as fast as the average

Overview

An *interpreter* translates spoken passages of a foreign language into another specified language. The job is often designated by the language interpreted, such as Spanish or Japanese. In addition, many interpreters specialize according to subject matter. For example, medical interpreters have extensive knowledge of and experience in the health care field, while court or judiciary interpreters speak both a second language and the "language" of the courts. Other interpreters aid in the communication between people who are unable to hear and those who can.

In contrast to interpreters, *translators* focus on written materials, such as books, plays, technical or scientific papers, legal documents, laws, treaties, and decrees. A sight translator performs a combination of interpreting and translating by reading printed material in one language while reciting it aloud in another.

History

Until recently, most people who spoke two languages well enough to interpret and translate did so only on the side, while working full time in some other occupation. For example, many diplomats and high-level government officials employed people who were able to serve as interpreters and translators should the need ever arise. However, such employees didn't spend much time performing only those services.

Interpreting and translating as professions have emerged only recently, partly in response to the need for high-speed communication across the globe. High-level diplomacy has also played a key role. For many years, diplomacy was practiced largely between two nations at a time. It was, therefore, rare that more than two languages were spoken at a conference table at any one time. The League of Nations, established by the Treaty of Versailles in 1919, established a new pattern of communication. For the first time, diplomatic discussions were carried out in many different languages, although the "language of diplomacy" was then considered to be French.

Since the early 1920s, multinational conferences of all kinds have become commonplace. Trade and educational conferences are now held with participants of many nations in attendance. Responsible for international diplomacy since the League of Nations has been dissolved, the United Nations now employs many full-time interpreters and translators, providing career opportunities for well-qualified people. In addition, the European Common Market (headquartered in Brussels, Belgium) employs a large number of interpreters.

The Job

Although interpreters are needed for a variety of languages in a myriad of venues and circumstances, there are only two basic systems of interpretation—simultaneous and consecutive. Simultaneous interpretation has been in use since the charter of the United Nations. In part, the invention and development of electronic sound equipment have made it possible.

Simultaneous interpreters are able to convert a spoken sentence that is still being completed in one language into another language. They may be so skillful that they are able to complete a sentence in the second language at almost the precise moment that the speaker is finishing the same sentence in the original language. Such interpreters are familiar with the speaking habits of the person whose speech is being interpreted and are thus able to anticipate the way in which the sentence will be completed. The interpreter may also make judgments about the intent of the sentence or phrase from the speaker's gestures, facial expressions, and inflections. At the same time, the interpreter must be careful not to summarize, edit, or in any way change what is being said.

In contrast, consecutive interpreters wait until the speaker has paused and then convert what the speaker has said to that point into the second language. The speaker must then wait until the interpreter has finished before beginning the next sentence. Since every sentence is repeated in consecutive interpretation, this method takes twice as long as does simultaneous interpretation.

For both systems, interpreters are placed so that they can clearly see and hear all that is taking place. In formal situations, such as those at the United Nations and other international conferences, interpreters are often assigned to a glass-enclosed booth. As speakers talk into a microphone, the sound is transmitted to this booth. The interpreter, in turn, talks into a microphone, translating the speaker's words into a second language. Each UN delegate, by manipulating the controls of a small electronic panel, can then tune in the voice of the interpreter who is speaking the most familiar language. Because of the difficulty of the job, these interpreters usually work in pairs. Two will be assigned to each booth and alternate in 30-minute shifts.

All international conference interpreters are simultaneous interpreters. Many interpreters, however, work in situations other than formal diplomatic meetings. For example, interpreters are needed for negotiations of all kinds, as well as for legal, financial, medical, and business interpreting. Court or judiciary interpreters, for example, work in courtrooms and at attorney-client meetings, depositions, and witness preparation sessions interpreting for people who can't communicate effectively in English.

Other interpreters serve "on call," traveling with visitors from foreign countries who are touring the United States. Usually, these language specialists employ consecutive interpretation. Their job is to make sure that the visitors are understood wherever they go and that they also understand what is being said to them. Still other interpreters accompany groups of U.S. citizens on official tours abroad. On such assignments, they may be sent to any foreign country and might be away from the United States for long periods of time.

Interpreters also work on short-term assignments. Services of an interpreter may be required for only brief intervals, such as for a single interview with representatives of the press or for an exchange of ideas with people whose opinions may be of interest to foreign visitors.

While interpreters focus on the spoken word, translators work with written language. They read and translate novels, plays, essays, nonfiction and technical works, legal documents, records and reports, speeches, and other written material. Translators generally follow a certain set of procedures in their work. They begin by reading text and making notes on what they do not understand. Then they look up words and terms in specialized dictionaries and glossaries to clarify the meaning of questionable passages. They may also do additional reading on the subject to arrive at a better understanding of it. Finally, they write a rough draft and then a final draft in the target language.

Requirements

High School

Since interpreting and translating are relatively new professional fields, there are no formal requirements for education or training, though preferences have been stated by employers. High school students interested in becoming interpreters or translators should take a variety of English courses, because they will probably be translating another language into English. In addition the study of one or more foreign languages is vital. If you're interested in becoming proficient in one or more of the Romance languages, basic courses in Latin will prove to be valuable.

While you should devote as much time as possible to the study of at least one modern foreign language, other helpful courses include speech, business, cultural studies, humanities, world history, geography, and political science. In fact, any course that emphasizes the written and/or spoken word will be valuable to aspiring interpreters or translators. In addition, knowledge of a particular subject matter, such as health, law, or science, in which you may have an interest, will give you a professional edge. Finally, courses in typing and word processing are recommended, especially if you want to pursue a career as a translator.

Postsecondary Training

Because interpreters and translators need to be proficient in grammar, have an excellent vocabulary in all of the languages spoken, and have sound knowledge in a wide variety of subjects, most employers require college degrees. In addition, scientific and professional interpreters are best qualified if they have achieved college and graduate degrees in the field in which they are to interpret. Many disciplines employ such highly technical language that it is difficult for someone who is not an expert in the field to comprehend the meaning of the terminology well enough to be able to convert it to another language.

In addition to language and field-specialty skills, you should take college courses that will allow you to develop effective techniques in public speaking, particularly if you're planning to pursue a career as an interpreter. Courses such as speech and debate will enable you to pay special attention to diction and work on the quality of your voice.

Many hundreds of colleges and universities in the United States offer bachelor's degrees in languages. In addition, a number of educational institutions now provide programs and degrees in interpreting and translating. The Georgetown University School of Languages and Linguistics, for example, offers a one- or two-year program of study in interpretation and translation. The Translation Studies Program at the University of Texas at Brownsville allows students to earn certificates in translation studies, translation and bilingual administration, or department interpretation. Graduate degrees in interpretation and translation may be earned at the University of California at Santa Barbara, the University of Puerto Rico, and the Monterey Institute of International Studies. Many of these programs include both general and specialized courses, such as medical interpretation and legal translation.

Europe provides academic programs for the training of interpreters as well. The University of Geneva's School of Interpreters is one such program. A diploma from this institution is greatly treasured by prospective interpreters.

Certification or Licensing

Although interpreters need not be certified to obtain a job, employers often show preference to certified applicants. Court interpreters who successfully pass a very strict written test may earn certification from the Administrative Office of the United States Courts, Washington, DC 20544. (As of 1995, these tests were being given for Spanish, Haitian Creole, and Navajo interpreters.) Deaf interpreters who pass an examination may qualify for either comprehensive or legal certification by the Registry of Interpreters for the Deaf (RID). Certain translators of foreign languages may be granted accreditation by the American Translators Association upon successful completion of that organization's required exams.

The U.S. Department of State has specific test requirements for its translators and interpreters. Three exams are offered: the nonprofessional escort interpreter, the lower level professional interpreter, and the higher-level professional interpreter. All exams are pass/fail. The requirements for application are several years of foreign language practice, advanced education in the language (preferably abroad), and fluency in vocabulary for a very broad range of subjects. It is extremely difficult to pass the exam with only an undergraduate degree and a year abroad for the study of the foreign language.

Other Requirements

Interpreters should be able to speak at least two languages fluently. They should speak without accent in each language and should know the languages so well that they do not need to consult dictionaries to find the particular meaning of an unusual word in the other language. In addition, both interpreters and translators should read daily newspapers in the languages in which they work to keep current in both developments and usage.

On a personal level, interpreters must have good hearing, a sharp mind, and a strong, clear, pleasant voice. They must be precise and quick in their translation. In addition to being flexible and versatile, both interpreters and translators should have self-discipline and patience. Above all, they should have an interest in and love of language and the word. Finally, they should observe confidentiality at all times—information they obtain in the process of interpretation or translation must never be passed along to unauthorized groups or people.

Exploring

If you have an opportunity to visit the United Nations, you can watch the proceedings to get some idea of the techniques and responsibilities of the job of the interpreter. Occasionally, an international conference session is televised, and the work of the interpreters can be observed. You should note, however, that interpreters who work at these conferences are in the top positions of the vocation. Not everyone may aspire to such jobs. The work of most interpreters is far less spectacular, but not necessarily less interesting.

If you have adequate skills in a foreign language, you might consider traveling in a country in which the language is spoken. If you can converse easily and without accent in that language and can interpret to others in the party who may not understand the language well, you can get a general idea of what an interpreter does.

Aspiring translators can communicate in another language and familiarize themselves with other cultures at the same time by regularly corresponding with a pen pal in a foreign country. You may also want to join a school club that focuses on a particular language, such as the French Club or the

Spanish Club. If there aren't any foreign language clubs at your school, you may want to form one. Such clubs allow you to hone your foreign language speaking and writing skills and learn about other countries and ways of life, too.

Finally, participation on the school debate team will allow you to practice your general speaking skills and improve your eye contact, gestures, facial expressions, tone, and other elements often used in interpreting.

Employers

Although many interpreters and translators work for government or international agencies, some are employed by private firms. Large import-export companies often have interpreters or translators on their payrolls, although these employees may also perform other duties for the firm. Large banks, companies that have overseas branches, organizations and associations that have international affiliates, and large communications and transportation firms often employ both interpreters and translators, with a translator director to coordinate their activities. In addition, translators and interpreters work at publishing houses, schools, bilingual newspapers, radio and television stations, airlines, shipping companies, law firms, and scientific and medical operations.

While translators are employed at a variety of venues nationwide, the highest percentage of interpreters finds work in New York and Washington, DC. Among the employers of interpreters and translators are the United Nations, the World Bank, the U.S. Department of State, the Bureau of the Census, the CIA, the FBI, the Library of Congress, the Red Cross, the YMCA, and the armed forces.

Finally, many interpreters and translators work in private practice. These self-employed professionals must be self-disciplined and driven, since they handle all aspects of the business, from scheduling work to billing clients.

Starting Out

Most interpreters and translators begin as part-time freelancers until they have enough experience to get regular staff jobs. Those who consider themselves to be already qualified can apply directly to the firm, agency, or organization for which they may wish to work. Many of these businesses advertise available positions in the classified section of the newspaper and on the Internet. In addition to checking with the college placement office, you should contact university language departments, which often get requests for qualified translators and interpreters.

Although the vocations of interpreting and translating are growing and the need for qualified professionals is increasing, top jobs are still hard to obtain and competition for them is fierce. The aspiring interpreter or translator may be wise to develop supplemental skills that can be used while perfecting interpreting and translating techniques and waiting for an opportunity to demonstrate competency in these areas. Such organizations as the United Nations employ secretaries who know two or more languages and who can take shorthand and transcribe notes in each of them. The United Nations also has a need for tour guides who speak more than one language well. Although secretarial and tour guide jobs may seem to have less prestige than the job of conference interpreter, such positions can be initial steps toward a worthwhile career goal.

Advancement

Competency in language determines the speed of advancement for interpreters and translators. Job opportunities and promotions into positions of responsibility are plentiful for those who have acquired great proficiency in languages. However, interpreters and translators need to constantly work and study to ensure that they keep abreast of current happenings in the countries in which their languages are spoken. Language changes constantly, as names for new inventions, machines, and processes are continuously being added. Those who do not keep up with language changes will find that their communication skills have become outdated.

Interpreters and translators who work for government agencies advance by clearly defined grade promotions. Those who work for other organizations can aspire to become chief interpreters or translators, reviewers who check the work of others, or staff directors.

Although advancement in the field is generally slow, interpreters and translators will find many opportunities to advance as freelancers. Some can even establish their own bureaus or agencies.

Earnings

Earnings for interpreters and translators vary, depending on experience, skills, number of languages used, and employers. Trainee interpreters working for the United States government earn between $19,700 and $25,700 a year. Those with college degrees may start at $24,500 to $31,800. Interpreters with advanced experience and training start at salaries that range from $29,900 to $47,000 per year. Senior interpreters working for the federal government earn starting salaries of about $55,000.

Interpreters employed by the United Nations work under a salary structure called the Common System. Those who work at the United Nations Headquarters in New York earn $21,300 to more than $53,000 a year. Top-ranking conference interpreters can earn an average annual income of more than $55,000 a year.

Freelance conference interpreters are paid from $350 (State Department) to $500 (private sector) a day. Most court interpreters also work on a freelance basis. While salaries vary, most of these professionals earn from $25,000 to $75,000 annually. Federally certified court interpreters (as well as qualified court interpreters in languages other than Spanish) are paid $250 per day, $135 for half days. Rates paid by state courts vary widely but are usually much lower.

Earnings are generally higher in private industry than in government. The United Nations and other international agencies pay higher rates than the U.S. government.

Trainee translators can expect to earn about $18,000 per year. Those who work on a freelance basis usually charge by the word, the page, the hour, or the project. Typical fees charged by freelancers begin at $0.10 per word. By the hour, translators usually earn between $15 and $35. Book translators work under contract with publishers. These contracts cover the fees that are to be paid for translating work as well as royalties, advances, penalties for late payments, and other provisions.

Depending on the employer, interpreters and translators often enjoy such benefits as health and life insurance, pension plans, and paid vacation and sick days.

Work Environment

Interpreters and translators work under a wide variety of circumstances and conditions. As a result, most do not have typical nine-to-five schedules.

Conference interpreters probably have the most comfortable physical facilities in which to work. Their glass-enclosed booths are well lit and temperature controlled. Court or judiciary interpreters work in courtrooms or conference rooms, while oral or deaf interpreters work at educational institutions as well as a wide variety of other locations.

Interpreters who work for escort or tour services are often required to travel for long periods of time. Their days begin and end in accordance with the group or person for whom they are interpreting. They follow the schedule of the group or person, attending the same meetings, eating at the same places, and traveling to the same sites. A freelance interpreter may work out of one city or be assigned anywhere in the world as needed.

Translators usually work in offices, although many spend considerable time in libraries and research centers. Freelance translators often work at home, using such tools of the trade as word processors, modems, dictionaries, and other resource materials.

While both interpreting and translating require flexibility and versatility, interpreters in particular, especially those who work at international banking firms or with international courts, may experience considerable stress and fatigue. Knowing that a great deal depends upon their absolute accuracy in interpretation is in itself tension-producing.

The ethical code of interpreters and translators is a rigid one. They must hold private proceedings in strict confidence. Ethics also demands that interpreters and translators not distort the meaning of the sentences that are spoken or written. No matter how much they may agree or disagree with the speaker or writer, they must be objective in the way in which they interpret or translate.

Outlook

Employment opportunities for interpreters and translators are expected to grow about as fast as the average. However, competition for available positions will be fierce. With the explosion of such technologies as the Internet, lightning-fast modems, ISDN, and videoconferencing, global communication has taken great strides. In short, the world has become smaller, so to speak, and the demand for translators and interpreters—both in the United States and abroad—is increasing.

In addition to new technologies, demographic factors will result in increased demand for translators and interpreters. Although some immigrants who come to the United States assimilate easily with respect to culture and language, many have difficulty with or do not want to learn English. As immigration into the country continues to increase, interpreters and translators will be needed to help immigrants understand what others are saying to them as well as to be understood. According to Ann Macfarlane, president-elect of the American Translators Association, "community interpreting" for immigrants and refugees is a challenging area requiring qualified language professionals.

Another demographic factor influencing the interpreting and translating fields is the aging of the baby boomers, those people born between 1946 and 1964. As the baby boomers retire, they will spend an increasing amount of money on travel, especially foreign travel. The resulting growth of the travel industry will create a need for interpreters to lead tours, both at home and abroad.

In addition to leisure travel, business travel is spurring the need for more translators and interpreters. With businesspeople traveling abroad in growing numbers to attend meetings, conferences, and seminars with clients and co-workers in foreign countries, interpreters and translators will be needed in growing numbers to bridge both the language gap and the cultural gap.

While no more than a few thousand simultaneous interpreters are employed in the three main markets (the federal government, international organizations, and organizations that work internationally, such as the Rotary Club), there are numerous opportunities for consecutive interpreters as well as for translators. The medical field, for example, provides a variety of jobs for language professionals, translating such products as pharmaceutical inserts, research papers, and medical reports for insurance companies. In addition, interpreters and translators will find opportunities in such areas as the law, trade and business, health care, tourism, recreation, and the government.

For More Information

American Association of Language Specialists
1000 Connecticut Avenue, NW, Suite 9
Washington, DC 20036
Tel: 301-986-1542

American Society of Interpreters
PO Box 9603
Washington, DC 20016
Tel: 703-883-0611

American Translators Association
1800 Diagonal Road, Suite 220
Alexandria, VA 22314
Tel: 703-683-6100
Web: http://www.atanet.org/

The Interpreters' Network
1326 Huron Street
London, Ontario, Canada N5V 2E2
Tel: 519-679-8473
Web: http://www.terpsnet.com/resources.htm

Magazine Editors

School Subjects
English
Journalism

Personal Interests
Communication/ideas
Helping/teaching

Work Environment
Primarily indoors
Primarily one location

Minimum Education Level
Bachelor's degree

Salary Range
$21,000 to $45,000 to $67,000+

Certification or Licensing
None available

Outlook
Faster than the average

Overview

Magazine editors plan the contents of a magazine, assign articles and select photographs and artwork to enhance the message of the articles, and edit, organize, and sometimes rewrite the articles. They are responsible for making sure that each issue is attractive, readable, and maintains the stylistic integrity of the publication. According to the *Occupational Outlook Handbook*, of the 286,000 writers and editors employed in 1996, a third worked for newspapers, magazines, and book publishers. Many major magazines are located in large metropolitan areas, but others are published throughout the country. (Also see *Editors*.)

The Job

The duties of a magazine editor are numerous, varied and unpredictable. The editor determines each article's placement in the magazine, working closely with the sales, art, and production departments to ensure that the publication's components complement each other and are appealing and readable.

Most magazines focus on a particular topic, such as fashion, news, or sports. Current topics of interest in the magazine's specialty area dictate a magazine's content. In some cases, magazines themselves set trends, generating interest in topics that become popular. Therefore, the editor should know the latest trends in the field that the magazine represents.

Depending on the magazine's size, editors may specialize in a particular area. For example, a fashion magazine may have a beauty editor, features editor, short story editor, and fashion editor. Each editor is responsible for acquiring, proofing, rewriting, and sometimes writing articles.

After determining the magazine's contents, the editor assigns articles to writers and photographers. The editor may have a clear vision of the topic or merely a rough outline. In any case, the editor supervises the article from writing through production, assisted by copy editors, assistant editors, fact checkers, researchers, and editorial assistants. The editor also sets a department budget and negotiates contracts with freelance writers, photographers, and artists.

The magazine editor reviews each article, checking it for clarity, conciseness, and reader appeal. Frequently, the editor edits the manuscript to highlight particular items. Sometimes the magazine editor writes an editorial to stimulate discussion or mold public opinion. The editor also may write articles on topics of personal interest.

Other editorial positions at magazines include the *editor-in-chief*, who is responsible for the overall editorial course of the magazine, the *executive editor*, who controls day-to-day scheduling and operations, and the *managing editor*, who coordinates copy flow and supervises production of master pages for each issue.

Some entry-level jobs in magazine editorial departments are stepping stones to more responsible positions. *Editorial assistants* perform various tasks such as answering phones and correspondence, setting up meetings and photography shoots, checking facts, and typing manuscripts. *Editorial production assistants* assist in coordinating the layout of feature articles edited by editors and art designed by art directors to prepare the magazine for printing.

Many magazines hire *freelance writers* to write articles on an assignment or contract basis. Most freelance writers write for several different publications; some become contributing editors to one or more publications to which they contribute the bulk of their work.

Magazines also employ *researchers,* sometimes called *fact checkers,* to ensure the factual accuracy of an article's content. Researchers may be on staff or hired on a freelance basis.

Requirements

Postsecondary Training

A college degree is required for entry into this field. A degree in journalism, English, or communications is the most popular and standard degree for a magazine editor. Specialized publications prefer a degree in the magazine's specialty, such as chemistry for a chemistry magazine, and experience in writing and editing. A broad liberal arts background is important for work at any magazine.

Most colleges and universities offer specific courses in magazine design, writing, editing, and photography. Related courses might include newspaper and book editing.

Other Requirements

All entry-level positions in magazine publishing require a working knowledge of typing and word processing, plus a superior command of grammar, punctuation, and spelling. Deadlines are important, so commitment, organization, and resourcefulness are crucial.

Editing is intellectually stimulating work that may involve investigative techniques in politics, history, and business. Magazine editors must be talented wordsmiths with impeccable judgment. Their decisions about which opinions, editorials, or essays to feature may influence a large number of people.

Employers

A mid-size special-interest publication (approximately 350,000 circulation) may employ an editorial staff of 12: editor-in-chief, executive editor, managing editor, art director, four associate editors, production manager, editorial assistant, assistant to the art director, and a clerical person.

An editor for a smaller magazine hires writers, oversees production, coordinates advertising with layout, and encourages increased subscriptions. Increasing subscriptions is a key goal, as businesses review these numbers and the targeted audience when deciding how to spend advertising dollars.

Major magazines are concentrated in New York, Chicago, Los Angeles, Boston, Philadelphia, San Francisco, and Washington, DC, while professional, technical, and union publications are spread throughout the country.

Earnings

In the 1990s, salaries for experienced editors ranged from $25,000 to $43,000; editorial assistants from $20,000 to $28,000; and supervisory editors, $33,000 to $57,200 per year. Senior editors at large-circulation magazines average more than $75,000 a year. In addition, many editors supplement their salaried income by doing freelance work.

Full-time editors receive vacation time, medical insurance and sick time, but freelancers must provide these for themselves.

Outlook

Magazine publishing is a dynamic industry. Magazines are launched every day of the year, although the majority fail. A recent trend in magazine publishing is focus on a special interest. There is increasing opportunity for employment at special-interest and trade magazines for those whose backgrounds complement a magazine's specialty. Association magazines, according to *Jobs '97*, offer potential employment opportunities. Magazine editing is keenly competitive, however, and as with any career, the applicant with the most education and experience has a better chance of getting the job.

For More Information

For general and summer internship program information, contact:

Magazine Publishers of America
919 Third Avenue, 22nd Floor
New York, NY 10022
Tel: 212-872-3700
Email: infocenter@magazine.org or asme@magazine.org
Web: http://www.magazine.org

Medical and Science Writers

English Journalism	School Subjects
Communication/ideas Technical/scientific	Personal Skills
Bachelor's degree	Minimum Education Level
$37,000 to $47,500 to $59,000	Salary Range
Voluntary	Certification or Licensing
Faster than the average	Outlook

Overview

Medical and science writers translate technical medical and scientific information so it can be disseminated to the general public and professionals in the field. Science and medical writers are involved with researching, interpreting, writing, and editing scientific and medical information. Their work often appears in books, technical studies and reports, magazine and trade journal articles, newspapers, company newsletters, on Web sites, and may be used for radio and television broadcasts.

History

The skill of writing has existed for thousands of years. Papyrus fragments with writing by ancient Egyptians date from about 3000 BC, and archaeological findings show that the Chinese had developed books by about 1300

BC. A number of technical obstacles had to be overcome before printing and the writing profession progressed.

The modern publishing age began in the 18th century. Printing became mechanized, and the novel, magazine, and newspaper developed. Developments in the printing trades, photoengraving, retailing, and the availability of capital produced a boom in newspapers and magazines in the 19th century. Further mechanization in the printing field, such as the use of the Linotype machine, high-speed rotary presses, and special color reproduction processes, set the stage for still further growth in the book, newspaper, and magazine industry.

In addition to the print media, the broadcasting industry has contributed to the development of the professional writer. Film, radio, and television are sources of entertainment, information, and education that provide employment for thousands of writers. Today, the computer industry, and the Internet and its proliferation of Web sites, have also created the need for more writers.

As our world has become more complex and people are seeking even more information, the professional writer has become increasingly important. And, as medicine and science are taking giant steps forward and discoveries are being made every day that impact our lives, skilled medical and science writers are needed to document these changes and disseminate the information.

The Job

Science or medical writers usually write about subjects related to these fields. Because the medical and scientific subject areas may sometimes overlap, writers often find that they do science writing as well as medical writing. For instance a medical writer might write about a scientific study that has an impact on the medical field.

Medical and science writing may be targeted for the printed page, the broadcast media, or the Web. It can be specific to one product and one type of writing, such as writing medical information and consumer publications for a specific drug line produced by a pharmaceutical company. Research facilities hire writers to edit reports or write about their scientific or medical studies. Writers who are public information officers write press releases that inform the public about the latest scientific or medical research findings. An educational publisher uses writers to write or edit educational materials for the medical profession. Medical and science writers also write online articles or interactive courses that are distributed over the Internet.

According to Barbara Gastel, M.D., coordinator of the Master of Science Program in Science and Technology Journalism at Texas A&M, many science and technology-related industries are using specialized writers to communicate complex subjects to the public. "In addition," she says, "opportunities exist in the popular media. Newspapers, radio, TV, and the Web have writers who specialize in covering medical and scientific subjects."

Medical and science writers usually write for the general public. They translate high-tech information into articles and reports that can be understood by the general public and the media. Good writers who cover the subjects thoroughly have inquisitive minds and enjoy looking for additional information that might add to their articles. They research the topic to gain a thorough understanding of the subject matter. This may require hours of research on the Internet, or in corporate, university, or public libraries. Writers always need good background information regarding a subject before they can write about it.

In order to get the information required, writers may interview professionals such as doctors, pharmacists, scientists, engineers, managers, and others familiar with the subject. Writers must know how to present the information so it can be understood. This requires knowing the audience and how to reach them. For example, an article may need graphs, photos, or historical facts. Writers sometimes enlist the help of technical or medical illustrators or engineers in order to add a visual dimension to their work.

For example, if reporting on a new heart surgery procedure that will soon be available to the public, writers may need to illustrate how that surgery is performed and what areas of the heart are affected. They may give a basic overview of how the healthy heart works, show a diseased heart in comparison, and report on how this surgery can help the patient. The public will also want to know how many people are affected by this disease, what the symptoms are, how many procedures have been done successfully, where they were performed, what the recovery time is, and if there are any complications. In addition, interviews with doctors and patients add a personal touch to the story.

Broadcast media need short, precise articles that can be transmitted in a specific time allotment. Writers usually need to work quickly because news-related stores are often deadline oriented. Because science and medicine can be so complex, medical and science writers also need to help the audience understand and evaluate the information. Writing for the Web encompasses most journalistic guidelines including time constraints and sometimes space constraints.

Some medical and science writers specialize in their subject matter. For instance, a medical writer may write only about heart disease and earn a reputation as the best writer in that subject area. Science writers may limit their writing or research to environmental science subjects, or may be even more specific and focus only on air pollution issues.

According to Jeanie Davis, president of the Southeast Chapter of the American Medical Writers Association, "Medical writing can take several different avenues. You may be a consumer medical writer, write technical medical research, or write about health care issues. Some choose to be medical editors and edit reports written by researchers. Sometimes this medical research must be translated into reports and news releases that the public can understand. Today many writers write for the Web." Davis adds, "It is a very dynamic profession, always changing."

Dr. Gastel says, "This career can have various appeals. People can combine their interest in science or medicine with their love of writing. It is a good field for a generalist who likes science and doesn't want to be tied to research in one area. Plus," she adds, "it is always fun to get things published."

Some writers may choose to be freelance writers either on a full- or part-time basis, or to supplement other jobs. Freelance science and medical writers are self-employed writers who work with small and large companies, health care organizations, research institutions, or publishing firms on a contract or hourly basis. They may specialize in writing about a specific scientific or medical subject for one or two clients, or they may write about a broad range of subjects for a number of different clients. Many freelance writers write articles, papers, or reports and then attempt to get them published in newspapers, trade, or consumer publications.

Requirements

High School

If you are considering a career as a writer, you should take English, journalism, and communication courses in high school. Computer classes will also be helpful. If you know in high school that you want to do scientific or medical writing, it would be to your advantage to take biology, physiology, chemistry, physics, math, health, and other science-related courses. If your school offers journalism courses and you have the chance to work on the school newspaper or yearbook, you should take advantage of this opportunity. Part-time employment at health care facilities, newspapers, publishing companies, or scientific research facilities can also provide experience and insight regarding this career. Volunteer opportunities are usually available in hospitals and nursing homes as well.

Postsecondary Training

Although not all writers are college-educated, today's jobs almost always require a bachelor's degree. Many writers earn an undergraduate degree in English, journalism, or liberal arts and then obtain a master's degree in a communications field such as medical or science writing. A good liberal arts education is important since you are often required to write about many subject areas. Science and medical-related courses are highly recommended. You should investigate internship programs that give you experience in the communications department of a corporation, medical institution, or research facility. Some newspapers, magazines, or public relations firms also have internships that give you the opportunity to write.

Some people find that after working as a writer, their interests are strong in the medical or science fields and they evolve into that writing specialty. They may return to school and enter a master's degree program or take some additional courses related specifically to science and medical writing. Similarly, science majors or people in the medical fields may find that they like the writing aspect of their jobs and return to school to pursue a career as a medical or science writer.

Certification or Licensing

Certification is not mandatory; however, certification programs are available from various organizations and institutions. The American Medical Writers Association Education Program offers an extensive continuing education and certification program.

Other Requirements

If you are considering a career as a medical or science writer, you should enjoy writing, be able to write well, and be able to express your ideas and those of others clearly. You should have an excellent knowledge of the English language and have superb grammar and spelling skills. You should be skilled in research techniques and be computer literate and familiar with software programs related to writing and publishing. You should be a curious person, enjoy learning about new things, and have an interest in science or medicine. You need to be detail-oriented since many of your writing assignments will require that you obtain and relay accurate and detailed information. Interpersonal skills are important too since many jobs require that you interact with and interview professional people such as scientists, engineers, researchers, and medical personnel. You must be able to meet deadlines and work under pressure.

Exploring

As a high school or college student, you can test your interest and aptitude in the field of writing by serving as a reporter or writer on school newspapers, yearbooks, and literary magazines. Attending writing workshops and taking writing classes will give you the opportunity to practice and sharpen your skills.

Community newspapers and local radio stations often welcome contributions from outside sources, although they may not have the resources to pay for them. Jobs in bookstores, magazine shops, libraries, and even newsstands offer a chance to become familiar with various publications. If you are interested in science writing, try to get a part-time job in a research laboratory, interview science writers, and read good science writing in major newspapers such as *The New York Times* or *The Wall Street Journal*. Similarly, if your interest is medical writing, work or volunteer in a health care facility, visit with people who do medical writing, and read medical articles in those newspapers previously listed.

Information on writing as a career may also be obtained by visiting local newspapers, publishing houses, or radio and television stations and interviewing some of the writers who work there. Career conferences and other guidance programs frequently include speakers from local or national organizations who can provide information on communication careers.

Some professional organizations such as the Society for Technical Communication welcome students as members and have special student membership rates and career information. In addition, participation in professional organizations gives you the opportunity to meet and visit with people in this career field.

Employers

Pharmaceutical and drug companies, medical research institutions, government organizations, insurance companies, health care facilities, nonprofit organizations, medical publishers, medical associations, and other medical-related industries employ medical writers.

Science writers may also be employed by medical-related industries. In addition, they are employed by scientific research companies, government research facilities, federal, state, and local agencies, manufacturing companies, research and development departments of corporations, and the chemical industries. Large universities and hospitals often employ science writers. Large technology-based corporations and industrial research groups also hire science writers.

Many medical and science writers are employed, often on a freelance basis, by newspapers, magazines, and the broadcast industries as well. Internet publishing is a growing field that hires science and medical writers. Corporations who deal with the medical or science industries also hire specialty writers as their public information officers or to head up communications departments within their facilities.

Starting Out

A fair amount of experience is required to gain a high-level position in this field. Most writers start out in entry-level positions. These jobs may be listed with college placement offices, or you may apply directly to the employment departments of corporations, institutions, universities, research facilities, nonprofit organizations, and government facilities that hire science and medical writers. Many firms now hire writers directly upon application or recommendation of college professors and placement offices. Want ads in newspapers and trade journals are another source for jobs. Serving an internship in college can give you the advantage of knowing people who can give you personal recommendations.

Internships are also excellent ways to build your portfolio. Employers in the communications field are usually interested in seeing samples of your published writing assembled in an organized portfolio or scrapbook. Working on your college's magazine or newspaper staff can help you build that portfolio. Sometimes small, regional magazines will also buy articles or assign short pieces for you to write. You should attempt to build your portfolio with good writing samples. Be sure to include the type of writing you are interested in doing, if possible.

You may need to begin your career as a junior writer or editor and work your way up. This usually involves library research, preparation of rough drafts for part or all of a report, cataloging, and other related writing tasks. These are generally carried on under the supervision of a senior writer.

Many science and medical writers enter the field after working in public relations departments, the medical profession, or science-related industries. They may use their skills to transfer to specialized writing positions or they may take additional courses or graduate work that focuses on writing or documentation skills.

Advancement

Writers with an undergraduate degree may choose to get a graduate degree in science or medical writing, corporate communications, document design, or a related program. An advanced degree may open doors to advanced careers.

Many experienced science and medical writers are often promoted to head writing, documentation, or public relations departments within corporations or institutions. Some may become recognized experts in their field and their writings may be in demand by trade journals, newspapers, magazines, and the broadcast industry.

As freelance writers prove themselves and work successfully with clients, they may be able to demand increased contract fees or hourly rates.

Earnings

Although there are no specific salary studies for science and medical writers, other writers' salary information is available.

The Society of Technical Communicators' 1999 salary survey of its members reported that the mean salary of its members was $47,560. The entry-level salary was reported to be $36,870, with the senior-level supervisor earning $58,970.

The Bureau of Labor Statistics reports that the mean annual wage for writers and editors in 1997 was $36,940. A survey of technical writers and editors conducted that same year showed that their pay was considerably higher. The mean annual wage for technical writers and editors was $41,740.

Freelance writers' earnings can vary depending on their expertise, reputation, and the articles they are contracted to write.

Most full-time writing positions offer the usual benefits such as insurance, sick leave, and paid vacation. Some jobs also provide tuition reimbursement and retirement benefits. Freelance writers must pay for their own insurance. However, there are professional associations that may offer group insurance rates for its members.

Work Environment

Work environment depends on the type of science or medical writing and the employer. Generally, writers work in an office or research environment. Writers for the news media sometimes work in noisy surroundings. Some writers travel to research information and conduct interviews while other employers may confine research to local libraries or the Internet. In addition, some employers require writers to conduct research interviews over the phone, rather than in person.

Although the workweek usually runs 35 to 40 hours in a normal office setting, many writers may have to work overtime to cover a story, interview people, meet deadlines, or to disseminate information in a timely manner. The newspaper and broadcasting industries deliver the news 24-hours a day, seven days a week. Writers often work nights and weekends to meet press deadlines or to cover a late-developing story.

Each day may bring new and interesting situations. Some stories may even take writers to exotic locations with a chance to interview famous people and write about timely topics. Other assignments may be boring or they may take place in less than desirable settings where interview subjects may be rude and unwilling to talk. One of the most difficult elements for writers may be meeting deadlines or gathering information. People who are the most content as writers work well with deadline pressure.

Outlook

According to the Bureau of Labor Statistics, there is a lot of competition for writing and editing jobs; however, the demand for writers and editors is expected to grow faster than the average until 2006.

The Society for Technical Communication also states that there is a growing demand for technical communicators. They report that it is one of the fastest growing professions and that this growth has created a variety of career options.

As we witness advances in medicine and science, we will continue to need skilled writers to relay that information to the public and other professionals.

For More Information

The following organizations provide information on careers as science and medical writers.

American Medical Writers Association
40 West Gude Drive, Suite 101
Rockville, MD 20850-1192
Tel: 301-294-5303
Web: http://www.amwa.org

National Association of Science Writers, Inc.
PO Box 294
Greenlawn, NY 11740
Tel: 516-757-5664
Web: http://www.nasw.org

The Society for Technical Communication offers student membership for persons enrolled in a program in preparation for a career in technical communication. This organization also has a scholarship program.

Society for Technical Communication
901 North Stuart Street, Suite 904
Arlington, VA 22203-1822
Tel: 703-522-4114
Web: http://www.stac-va.org

Newspaper Editors

School Subjects
English
Journalism

Personal Interests
Communication/ideas
Helping/teaching

Work Environment
Primarily indoors
Primarily one location

Minimum Education Level
Bachelor's degree

Salary Range
$21,000 to $45,000 to $67,000+

Certification or Licensing
None available

Outlook
Faster than the average

Overview

Newspaper editors assign, review, edit, rewrite, and lay out copy in a newspaper—everything except advertisements. Editors sometimes write stories or editorials that offer opinions on issues. Editors review the editorial page and copy written by staff or syndicated columnists. A large metropolitan daily newspaper staff may include various editors who process thousands of words into print daily. A small-town weekly paper staff, however, may include only one editor, who might be both owner and star reporter. According to the *Occupational Outlook Handbook,* of the 286,000 writers and editors employed in 1996, a third worked for newspapers, magazines, and book publishers. According to *Jobs '97,* 59,000 of the 75,000 journalists worked for newspapers. Large metropolitan areas—New York, Washington, DC, Los Angeles, and Chicago—employ many editors. (Also see *Editors.*)

The Job

Newspaper editors are responsible for the paper's entire news content. The news section includes features, "hard" news and editorial commentary. Editors of a daily paper plan the contents of each day's issue, assigning articles, reviewing submissions, prioritizing stories, checking wire services, selecting illustrations, and laying out each page with the advertising space allotted.

At a large daily newspaper, an *editor-in-chief* oversees the entire editorial operation, determines its editorial policy, and reports to the publisher. The *managing editor* is responsible for day-to-day operations in an administrative capacity. *Story editors,* or *wire editors,* determine which national news agency (or wire service) stories will be used and edit them. Wire services give smaller papers, without foreign correspondents, access to international stories.

A *city editor* gathers local and sometimes state and national news. The city editor hires copy editors and reporters, hands out assignments to reporters and photographers, reviews and edits stories, confers with executive editors on story content and space availability, and gives stories to copy editors for final editing.

A newspaper may have separate desks for state, national, and foreign news, each with its own head editor. Some papers have separate editorial page editors. The *department editors* oversee individual features; they include business editors, fashion editors, sports editors, book section editors, entertainment editors, and more. Department heads make decisions on coverage, recommend story ideas, and make assignments. They often have backgrounds in their department's subject matter and are highly skilled at writing and editing.

The copy desk, the story's last stop, is staffed by *copy editors,* who correct spelling, grammar, and punctuation mistakes; check for readability and sense; edit for clarification; examine stories for factual accuracy; and ensure the story conforms to editorial policy. Copy editors sometimes write headlines or picture captions and may crop photos. Occasionally they find serious problems that cause them to kick stories back to the editors or the writer.

Editors, particularly copy editors, base many decisions on a style book that provides preferences in spelling, grammar, and word usage; it indicates when to use foreign spellings or English translations and the preferred system of transliteration. Some houses develop their own style books, but often they use or adapt the *Associated Press Stylebook and Libel Manual.*

After editors approve the story's organization, coverage, writing quality, and accuracy, they turn it over to the *news editors,* who supervise article placement and determine page layout with the advertising department. News and *executive editors* discuss the relative priorities of major news stories. If a paper is divided into several sections, each has its own priorities.

Modern newspaper editors depend heavily on computers. Generally, a reporter types the story directly onto the computer network, providing editors with immediate access. Some editorial departments are situated remotely from printing facilities, but computers allow the printer to receive copy immediately upon approval. Today designers computerize page layout. Many columnists send their finished columns from home computers to the editorial department via modem.

Requirements

Postsecondary Training

According to *Jobs '97,* nearly 85 percent of first-time journalists had journalism or mass communications degrees. Newspapers hired 75 percent of their staffs from other newspapers or media, 25 percent from colleges; 78 percent worked at college newspapers, 83 percent as interns.

Prospective editors should find a school with strong journalism and communications programs. Many require two years of liberal arts studies before journalism study. Journalism courses include reporting, writing, and editing; press law and ethics; journalism history; and photojournalism. Advanced classes include feature writing, investigative reporting, and graphics. Some schools offer internships for credit.

Newspapers look closely at extracurricular activities, emphasizing internships, school newspaper and freelance writing and editing, and part-time newspaper work (stringing). Typing, computer skills, and knowledge of printing are helpful.

Employers

Generally there is employment for editors in every city or town, as most towns have at least one newspaper. As the population multiplies, so do the opportunities. In large metropolitan areas, there may be one or two dailies, several general interest weeklies, ethnic and other special-interest weeklies or monthlies, trade newspapers, and daily and weekly community and suburban newspapers, most with managing and department editors.

Earnings

Newspaper editors' salaries vary from small to large communities, but newspaper people generally are well compensated. Other factors affecting compensation include quality of education and previous experience, job level, and the newspaper's circulation. Large metropolitan dailies offer higher paying jobs, while outlying weekly papers pay less. According to the *Occupational Outlook Handbook,* beginning writers and editorial assistants average $21,000 annually while those with five or more years of experience earn more than $30,000. Senior editors at large newspapers earn more than $67,000 annually. Salary ranges and benefits for most nonmanagerial editorial workers, including editors and reporters, on many newspapers are negotiated by the Newspaper Guild.

Outlook

According to the *Occupational Outlook Handbook,* employment of editors and writers, while highly competitive, should be faster than the average through 2006. Opportunities will be better on small daily and weekly newspapers, where the pay is lower. Some publications hire freelance editors to support reduced full-time staffs. And as experienced editors leave the workforce or move to other fields, job openings will occur.

For More Information

ASNE helps editors improve their craft, and better serve their communities. It preserves and promotes core journalistic values.

American Society of Newspaper Editors
11690B Sunrise Valley Drive
Reston, VA 20191-1409
Tel: 703-453-1122
Web: http://www.asne.org

Founded in 1958 by the Wall Street Journal *to improve the quality of journalism education, this organization offers internships, scholarships, and literature for college students.* For information on how to receive a copy of *The Journalist's Road to Success, which lists schools offering degrees in news-editorial and financial aid to those interested in print journalism, contact:*

Dow Jones Newspaper Fund
PO Box 300
Princeton, NJ 08543-0300
Tel: 609-452-2820
Email: newsfund@wsj.dowjones.com
Web: http://www.dj.com/newsfund

To receive a free copy of Newspaper: What's in it for Me? *write:*

Newspaper Careers Project
Fulfillment Department, NAA Foundation
11600 Sunrise Valley Drive
Reston, VA 22091

This trade association for African-American-owned newspapers has a foundation that offers a scholarship and internship program for inner-city high school juniors.

National Newspaper Publishers Association
3200 13th Street, NW
Washington, DC 20010
Tel: 202-588-8764
Email: nnpadc@nnpa.org
Web: http://www.nnpa.org

This organization for journalists has campus and online chapters.

Society of Professional Journalists
16 South Jackson
Greencastle, IN 46135-0077
Tel: 765-653-3333
Email: spj@link2000.net
Web: http://spj.org/spjhome.htm

Press Secretaries

English Government Journalism	School Subjects
Communication/ideas Leadership/management	Personal Skills
Primarily indoors One location with some travel	Work Environment
Bachelor's degree	Minimum Education Level
$47,000 to $150,000 to $200,000+	Salary Range
None available	Certification or Licensing
About as fast as the average	Outlook

Overview

Press secretaries, political consultants, and other media relations professionals help politicians promote themselves and their issues among voters. They advise politicians on how to address the media. Sometimes considered "spin doctors," these professionals use the media to either change or strengthen public opinion. Press secretaries work for candidates and elected officials, while political consultants work with firms, contracting their services to politicians. The majority of press secretaries and political consultants work in Washington, DC; others work all across the country, involved with local and state government officials and candidates.

History

Using the media for political purposes is nearly as old as the U.S. government itself. The news media developed right alongside the political parties, and early newspapers served as a battleground for the Federalists and the Republicans. The first media moguls of the late 1800s often saw their newspapers as podiums from which to promote themselves—George Hearst bought the *San Francisco Examiner* in 1885 for the sole purpose of helping him campaign for Congress. The latter half of the 20th century introduced whole other forms of media, which were quickly exploited by politicians seeking offices. Many historians mark the Kennedy-Nixon debate of 1960 as the moment when television coverage first became a key factor in the election process. Those who read of the debate in the next day's newspapers were under the impression that Nixon had easily won, but it was Kennedy's composure and appeal on camera that made the most powerful impression. Negative campaigning first showed its powerful influence in 1964, when Democratic presidential candidate Lyndon Johnson ran ads featuring a girl picking a flower while a nuclear bomb burst in the background, which commented on Republican Barry Goldwater's advocacy of strong military action in Vietnam.

Bill Clinton is probably the first president to benefit from the art of "spin," as his press secretaries and political managers were actively involved in dealing with his scandals and keeping his approval ratings high among the population. James Carville and George Stephanopolis, working for Clinton's 1992 campaign, had the task of playing up Clinton's strengths as an intelligent, gifted politician, while down-playing his questionable moral background. Their efforts were portrayed in the documentary *The War Room*, and their success earned them national renown as "spin doctors."

The Job

If you were to manage a political campaign, how would you go about publicizing the candidate to the largest number of voters? You'd use TV, of course. The need for TV and radio spots during a campaign is the reason it costs so much today to run for office. And it's also the reason many politicians hire professionals with an understanding of media relations to help them get elected. Once elected, a politician continues to rely on media relations experts, such as press secretaries, political consultants, and political managers, to use the media to portray the politician in the best light. In recent years, such words as "spin," "leak," and "sound-bite" have entered the daily vocabulary of news and politics to describe elements of political coverage in the media.

Political consultants usually work independently, or as members of consulting firms, and contract with individuals. As a political consultant, you're involved in producing radio and TV ads, writing campaign plans, and developing "themes" for these campaigns. A theme may focus on a specific issue or on the differences between your client and the opponent. Your client may be new to the political arena or someone established looking to maintain an office. You conduct polls and surveys to gauge public opinion and to identify your client's biggest competition. You advise your clients in the best ways to use the media. In addition to TV and radio, the Internet has proven important to politicians. Consultants launch campaign Web sites and also chase down rumors that spread across the Internet. A consultant may be hired for an entire campaign, or may be hired only to produce an ad, or to come up with a "sound-bite"—or catchy quote—for the media.

Though voters across the country complain about negative campaigning, or "mud-slinging," such campaigns have proven effective. In his 1988 presidential campaign, George Bush ran TV ads featuring the now notorious Willie Horton, a convict who was released from prison only to commit another crime. The ad was intended to draw attention to what Bush considered his opponent's "soft" approach to crime. It proved very effective in undermining the campaign of Michael Dukakis and putting him on the defensive. Many consultants believe they must focus on a few specific issues in a campaign, emphasizing their client's strengths as well as the opponent's weaknesses.

Press secretaries serve on the congressional staffs of senators and representatives and on the staffs of governors and mayors. The president also has a press secretary. Press secretaries and their assistants write press releases and opinion pieces to publicize the efforts of the government officials for whom they work. They also help prepare speeches and prepare their employers for press conferences and interviews. They maintain Web sites, posting press releases and the results of press conferences.

Media relations experts are often called spin doctors because of their ability to manipulate the media, or put a good spin on a news story to best suit the purposes of their clients. Corporations also rely on spin for positive media coverage. Media relations experts are often called upon during a political scandal, or after corporate blunders, for "damage control." Using the newspapers and radio and TV broadcasts, spin doctors attempt to downplay public relations disasters, helping politicians and corporations save face. In highly sensitive situations, they must answer questions selectively and carefully, and they may even be involved in secretly releasing, or leaking, information to the press. Because of these manipulations, media relations professionals are often disrespected. They're sometimes viewed as people who conceal facts and present lies, prey on the emotions of voters, or even represent companies responsible for illegal practices. However, many political consultants and media representatives are responsible for bringing public attention to important issues and good political candidates. They also help organizations and nonprofit groups advocate for legislative issues and help develop support for school funding, environmental concerns, and other community needs.

Requirements

High School

Take journalism courses, and work with your school newspaper, radio station, or TV station—you'll recognize how important reporters, editors, and producers are in putting together newspapers and shaping news segments. English composition, drama, and speech classes will help you develop good communication skills, while government, history, and civics classes will teach you about the structure of local, state, and federal government. Join your speech and debate team, and you'll gain experience in research and in persuasive argument. Take math, economics, and accounting courses to prepare you for poll-taking and for analyzing statistics and demographics.

Postsecondary Training

Most people in media relations have bachelor's degrees, and some also hold master's degrees, doctorates, and law degrees. As an undergraduate, you should enroll in a four-year college and pursue a well-rounded education; press secretaries and political consultants need a good understanding of the history and culture of the United States and foreign countries. Some of the majors you should consider as an undergraduate are journalism, political science, English, marketing, and economics. You'll also take courses in government, psychology, statistics, history of western civilization, and a foreign language. You might then choose to pursue a graduate degree in journalism, political science, public administration, or international relations.

Seek a college with a good internship program. You might also pursue internships with local and state officials and your congressional members in the Senate and House of Representatives. Journalism internships will involve you with local and national publications, or the news departments of radio and TV stations.

The American Association of Political Consultants (AAPC) does have a code of conduct for consultants, but there is no established training or licensing process.

Other Requirements

You'll need to be very organized and capable of juggling many different tasks, from quickly writing ads and press releases to developing budgets and expense accounts. You'll need good problem-solving skills and some imagination when putting a positive spin on negative issues. Good people skills are important so that you can develop contacts within government and the media. You should feel comfortable with public speaking as you'll be leading press conferences and speaking on behalf of your employers and clients. You should also enjoy competition. You can't be intimidated by people in power or by journalists questioning the issues addressed in your campaigns.

Exploring

Get involved with your school government as well as with committees and clubs that have officers and elections. You can also become involved in local, state, and federal elections by volunteering for campaigns; though you may just be making phone calls and putting up signs, you may also have the opportunity to write press releases and schedule press conferences and interviews, and you'll see first-hand how a campaign operates.

Working for your school newspaper will help you learn about conducting research, interviews, and opinion polls, which all play a part in managing media relations. You may be able to get a part-time job or an internship with your city's newspaper or broadcast news station, where you'll gain experience with election coverage and political advertising. Visit the Web sites of U.S. Congress members; many sites feature lists of recent press releases. By reading the press releases, you'll get a sense of how a press office publicizes the efforts and actions of congressional members. You should also read some of the many books examining recent political campaigns and scandals, and read magazines like *Harper's, Atlantic Monthly, George,* and the online magazine *Salon,* for political commentary.

Employers

Press secretaries work for local, state, and federal government officials. Political consultants are generally self-employed, or work for consulting firms that specialize in media relations. You might also find work with public relations agencies, and the press offices of large corporations. Celebrities, and others in the public eye also hire press agents to help them control rumors and publicity. Political consultants contract with politicians, corporations, nonprofit groups, and trade and professional associations. They participate in the campaigns of mayors, governors, and congressional members as well as in the political campaigns of other countries. Someone like the president will keep in close contact with many different media advisors, including his or her current and former press secretaries, consultants, speechwriters, and political managers.

Starting Out

Media relations jobs aren't advertised, and there's no predetermined path to success. You'll find your way in the field by making connections with people in both politics and the media. Volunteer for political campaigns, and also advocate for public policy issues of interest to you. You can make good connections, and gain valuable experience, working or interning in the offices of your state capitol. You might also try for an internship with one of your state's members of Congress; contact their offices in Washington, DC, for internship applications. If you're more interested in the writing and producing aspects of the career, work for local newspapers or the broadcast news media; or work as a producer for a television production crew or for an ad agency that specializes in political campaigns. A political consulting firm may hire assistants for writing and for commercial production. Whereas some people pursue the career directly by working in the press offices of political candidates, others find their way into political consulting after having worked as lawyers, lobbyists, or journalists.

Advancement

A press secretary who has worked closely with a successful government official may advance into a higher staff position, like chief of staff or legislative director. Political consultants, after winning many elections and establishing credentials, will begin to take on more prominent clients and major campaigns. Network TV, cable, and radio news departments also hire successful media relations experts to serve as political analysts on the air. Some consultants also write columns for newspapers and syndicates and publish books about their insights into politics.

Earnings

Press secretaries working in the U.S. Congress can make between $42,000 and $60,000 a year, according to the Congressional Management Foundation, a consulting firm in Washington, DC. The incomes of political consultants vary greatly; someone contracting with local candidates, or with state organizations and associations, may make around $40,000 a year; someone consulting with high-profile candidates may bring in hundreds of thousands of dollars a year. In 1998, the Pew Research Center released the results of one of the first comprehensive studies of political consultants. More than half of its respondents reported family incomes of more than $150,000 a year; one-third reported annual incomes of more than $200,000.

Work Environment

Representing politicians can be thankless work. You may have to speak to the press about sensitive, volatile issues and deal directly with the frustrations of journalists unable to get the answers they want. When working for prominent politicians, you may become the subject of personal attacks.

Despite these potential conflicts, your work can be exciting and fast-paced. You'll see the results of your efforts in the newspapers and television, and you'll have the satisfaction of influencing voters and public opinion. If working on a campaign as a consultant, your hours will be long and stressful. In some cases, you'll have to scrap unproductive media ads and start from scratch with only hours to write, produce, and place new commercials. You'll also have to be available to your clients around the clock.

Though a majority of press secretaries and political consultants work in Washington, DC, others work in state capitols and major cities all across the country.

Outlook

Consultants and media representatives will become increasingly important to candidates and elected officials. Television ads and Internet campaigns have become almost necessary to reach the public. The work of press secretaries will expand as more news networks and news magazines more closely follow the decisions and actions of government officials.

The Pew Research Center, which surveys public opinion on political issues, has found that most Americans are concerned about negative campaigning, while most political consultants see nothing wrong with using negative tactics in advertising. Despite how the general public may feel about negative campaigning, it remains a very effective tool for consultants. In some local elections, candidates may mutually agree to avoid the mud-slinging, but the use of negative ads in general is likely to increase.

This negative campaigning may be affected somewhat by developing technology. Voters will soon be able to access more information about candidates and issues via the Internet. Also, the increase in the number of channels available to cable TV watchers will make it more difficult for candidates to advertise to a general audience. However, the greater number of outlets for media products will employ more writers, TV producers, and Web designers in the process of creating a political campaign.

For More Information

Visit the Web sites of the House and the Senate for links to the Web sites of individual members of Congress. At the Web sites, you can read press releases.

Office of Senator (Name)
United States Senate
Washington, DC 20510
Tel: 202-224-3121
Web: http://www.senate.gov

U.S. House of Representatives (Name)
Washington, DC 20515
Tel: 202-224-3121
Web: http://www.house.gov

For general information about careers in broadcast media, contact:

National Association of Broadcasters
1771 N Street, NW
Washington, DC 20036
Tel: 202-429-5335
Web: http://www.nab.org/

The Pew Research Center is an opinion research group that studies attitudes toward press, politics, and public policy issues. To read some of their survey results, visit their Web site, or write:

The Pew Research Center for the People and the Press
1150 18th Street, NW, Suite 975
Washington, DC 20036
Tel: 202-293-3126
Web: http://www.people-press.org

Public Relations Specialists

School Subjects
Business
English
Journalism

Personal Skills
Leadership/management
Communication/ideas

Work Environment
Primarily indoors
One location with some travel

Minimum Education Level
Bachelor's degree

Salary Range
$15,000 to $50,000 to $150,000

Certification or Licensing
None available

Outlook
Faster than the average

Overview

Public relations specialists develop and maintain programs that present a favorable public image for an individual or organization. They provide information to the target audience (generally, the public at large) about the client, its goals and accomplishments, and any further plans or projects that may be of public interest.

According to the Public Relations Society of America (PRSA), there are approximately 110,000 public relations professionals in the United States. PR specialists may be employed by corporations, government agencies, nonprofit organizations—almost any type of organization. Many PR specialists hold positions in public relations consulting firms or work for advertising agencies. PRSA reports that there are between 7,200 and 12,000 public relations providers, including firms and sole practitioners, in the United States. Most public relations firms are located in large cities, such as New York, Chicago, Los Angeles, and Washington, DC.

History

The first public relations counsel was a reporter named Ivy Ledbetter Lee, who in 1906 was named press representative for coal-mine operators. Labor disputes were becoming a large concern of the operators, and they had run into problems because of their continual refusal to talk to the press and the hired miners. Lee convinced the mine operators to start responding to press questions and supply the press with information on the mine activities.

During and after World War II, the rapid advancement of communications techniques prompted firms to realize the need for professional help to ensure their messages were given proper public attention. Manufacturing firms that had turned their productive facilities over to the war effort returned to the manufacture of peacetime products and enlisted the aid of public relations professionals to bring products and the company name forcefully before the buying public.

Large business firms, labor unions, and service organizations, such as the American Red Cross, Boy Scouts of America, and the YMCA, began to recognize the value of establishing positive, healthy relationships with the public that they served and depended on for support. The need for effective public relations was often emphasized when circumstances beyond a company's or institution's control created unfavorable reaction from the public.

Public relations specialists must be experts at representing their clients before the media. The rapid growth of the public relations field since 1945 is testimony to the increased awareness in all industries of the need for professional attention to the proper use of media and the proper public relations approach to the many publics of a firm or an organization—customers, employees, stockholders, contributors, and competitors.

The Job

Public relations specialists are concerned with one or more of the following types of work: writing reports, news releases, booklet texts, speeches, copy for radio, TV, and film sequences; editing employee publications, newsletters, shareholder reports, and other management communications; contacting the press, radio, and TV as well as magazines on behalf of the employer; handling special events, such as press parties, convention exhibits, open houses, new facility, or anniversary celebrations; making appearances before groups and selecting appropriate platforms for company officers; using a background knowledge of art and layout for developing brochures, booklets, and photographic communications; programming and determining the public relations needs of the employer, defining the goals of the public relations effort, and recommending steps to carry out the program; and supervising the advertising of a company's or an institution's name and reputation as opposed to advertising a company's wares.

The public relations executive consults with management on company behavior to ensure that the company or institution conducts itself in a way that merits public confidence. Public relations workers are alert to any and all company or institutional events that are newsworthy. They prepare news releases and direct them toward the proper media. Public relations specialists working for manufacturers and retailers are concerned with efforts that will promote sales and create goodwill for the firm's products. They work closely with the marketing and sales departments in announcing new products, preparing displays, and attending occasional dealers' conventions.

A large firm may have a director of public relations who is a vice president of the company and in charge of a staff that includes writers, artists, researchers, and other specialists. Publicity for an individual or a small organization may involve many of the same areas of expertise but be carried out by only a few people or possibly one person.

Many public relations people work as consultants, rather than as members of the staff of a corporation, college, or hospital. As staff members of a consulting firm, they have the advantage of being able to operate independently, state opinions objectively, and work with more than one type of business or association.

Public relations people are called upon to work with the public opinion aspects of almost every corporate or institutional problem. These can range from a plant opening to a dormitory dedication, from a merger or sale of a subsidiary to the condemnation of land for campus expansion.

Public relations professionals may specialize. Lobbyists try to persuade legislators and other office holders to pass laws favoring the interests of the firms or people they represent. Fund-raising directors develop and direct programs designed to raise funds for social welfare agencies and other nonprofit organizations.

Early in their careers, public relations specialists become accustomed to having others receive credit for their behind-the-scenes work. The speeches they draft will be delivered by company officers, the magazine articles they prepare may be credited to the president of the company, and they may be consulted to prepare the message to stockholders from the chairman of the board that appears in the annual report.

Requirements

High School

Interested high school students should take courses in English, journalism, public speaking, humanities, and languages because public relations is based on effective communication with others. Courses such as these will help to develop skills in written and oral communication as well as provide a better understanding of different fields and industries to be publicized.

Postsecondary Training

Most people employed in public relations service have a college degree. Major fields of study most beneficial to developing the proper skills are public relations, English, and journalism. Some employers feel that majoring in the area in which the public relations person will eventually work (for example, a science degree) is the best training. A knowledge of business administration is most helpful as is a native talent for selling. A graduate degree may be required for managerial positions, while people with a bachelor's degree in public relations find staff positions with either an organization or a public relations firm.

In 1996, more than 200 colleges and about 100 graduate schools offered degree programs or special courses in public relations. In addition, many other colleges offered at least one course in the field. Public relations programs are sometimes administered by the journalism or communication departments of schools. In addition to courses in theory and techniques of public relations, interested individuals may study organization, management and administration, and practical applications and often specialize in areas such as business, government, and nonprofit organizations. Other preparation includes courses in creative writing, psychology, communications, advertising, and journalism.

Certification or Licensing

The Public Relations Society of America and the International Association of Business Communicators accredit public relations workers who have passed a comprehensive examination. Such accreditation is a sign of competence in this field, although it is not a requirement for employment.

Other Requirements

Today's public relations specialist must be a businessperson first, both to understand how to perform successfully in business and to comprehend the needs and goals of the organization or client. Additionally, the public relations specialist needs to be a strong writer and speaker, with good interpersonal, leadership, and organizational skills.

Exploring

Almost any experience in working successfully with other people will help students seeking opportunities in the field of public relations to develop strong interpersonal skills, which are crucial in public relations. Summer work on a newspaper or a PR trade paper or a job with a radio or television station may give insight into communications media. Work as a volunteer on a political campaign can help students understand the ways in which people can be persuaded. Being selected as a page for the U.S. Congress or a state legislature may help students grasp the fundamentals of government processes. A job in retail will help them understand some of the principles of product presentation; a teaching job will help them organize their presentation in a logical way.

Employers

Public relations workers may be paid employees of the organization they represent or they may be part of a public relations firm that works for organizations on a contract basis. Others are involved in fund-raising or political campaigning. Public relations may be done for a corporation, retail business, service company, utility, association, nonprofit organization, or educational institution.

Most PR firms are located in large cities that are centers of communications. The main offices of most large industries or associations are also in these same large cities, and it is from these offices that the public relations department functions. New York, Chicago, Los Angeles, and Washington, DC, are good places to start a search for a public relations job. Nevertheless, there are many good opportunities in cities across the United States.

According to "Corporate Communications Benchmark—1997," a major research initiative sponsored by Edelman Public Relations Worldwide, Opinion Research Corporation, and the Integrated Marketing Communications Department of Northwestern University's Medill School of Journalism, nearly 90 percent of the 100 major companies surveyed used external communications agencies at corporate headquarters, while only 5 percent reported that their companies did not use any outside agency. Results of this study were reported in IABC's Communication World Online in July 1997.

Starting Out

There is no clear-cut formula for getting a job in public relations. A person often enters the field after gaining preliminary experience in another occupation closely allied to the field, usually some segment of communications, and frequently, in journalism. Coming into public relations from newspaper work is still a recommended route. Another good method is to gain initial employment as a public relations trainee or intern, or as a clerk, secretary, or research assistant in a public relations department or a counseling firm.

Advancement

In some large companies, an entry-level public relations specialist may start as a trainee in a formal training program for new employees. In others, new employees may expect to be assigned to work that has a minimum of responsibility. They may assemble clippings or do rewrites on material that has already been accepted. They may make posters or assist in conducting polls or surveys, or compile reports from data submitted by others.

As workers acquire experience, they are given more responsibility. They write news releases, direct polls or surveys, or advance to writing speeches for company officials. Progress may seem to be slow, because some skills take a long time to master.

Some advance in responsibility and salary in the same firm in which they started. Others find that the path to advancement is to accept a more attractive position in another firm.

The goal of many public relations specialists is to open an independent office or to join an established consulting firm. To start an independent office requires a large outlay of capital and an established reputation in the field. However, those who are successful in operating their own consulting firms probably attain the greatest financial success in the public relations field.

Earnings

A beginning public relations salary might be about $15,000 a year, but within a few years it can increase to $21,000 or more, according to the Public Relations Society of America. Public relations specialists have median annual earnings of about $50,000. Top salaries generally approach $150,000.

According to a 1997 salary survey conducted by the International Association of Business Communicators, account executives in the United States had median salaries of $36,000 and averaged $38,549; specialists had median salaries of $38,300 and averaged $39,287; and independent or self-employed public relations professionals had median salaries of $40,000 and averaged $46,124. Public affairs specialists in the federal government averaged about $52,240 in 1996.

According to a 1996 study by executive search firm Marshall Consultants, as reported in IABC's Communication World Online, overall compensation for communications professionals rose 5 to 8 percent. The study also found that investor relations professionals earn higher-than-average incomes, as do media relations specialists, and communicators in the fields of high technology and health care also earn higher incomes. Geographically, compensation was found to be higher in the northeastern United States, especially the New York metropolitan area and other urban areas.

Many PR workers receive a range of fringe benefits from corporations and agencies employing them, including bonus/incentive compensation, stock options, profit sharing/pension plans/401(k) programs, medical benefits, life insurance, financial planning, maternity/paternity leave, paid vacations, and family college tuition. Bonuses can range from 5 to 100 percent of base compensation and often are based on individual and/or company performance.

Work Environment

Public relations specialists generally work in offices with adequate secretarial help, regular salary increases, and expense accounts. They are expected to make a good appearance in tasteful, conservative clothing. They must have social poise, and their conduct in their personal life is important to their firms or their clients. The public relations specialist may have to entertain business associates.

The public relations person seldom works the conventional office hours for many weeks at a time; although the workweek may consist of 35 to 40 hours, these hours may be supplemented by evenings and even weekends when meetings must be attended and other special events covered. Time behind the desk may represent only a small part of the total working schedule. Travel is often an important and necessary part of the job.

The life of the public relations executive is so greatly determined by the job that many consider this a disadvantage. Because public relations is concerned with public opinion, it is often difficult to measure the results of performance and to sell the worth of a public relations program to an employer or client. Competition in the consulting field is keen, and if a firm loses an account, some of its personnel may be affected. The demands it makes for anonymity will be considered by some as one of the profession's less inviting aspects. Public relations involves much more hard work and a great deal less glamour than is popularly supposed.

Outlook

According to the Public Relations Society of America, employment of public relations professionals is expected to grow faster than average for all other occupations through the year 2006, according to the U.S. Department of Labor. Competition will be keen for beginning jobs in public relations because so many job seekers are enticed by the perceived glamour and appeal of the field; those with both education and experience will have an advantage.

Most large companies have some sort of public relations resource, either through their own staff or through the use of a firm of consultants. They are expected to expand their public relations activities and create many new jobs. More of the smaller companies are hiring public relations specialists, adding to the demand for these workers.

According to the study by Marshall Consultants (published in IABC's Communication World Online in July 1997), the 1996 surge in hiring and today's low unemployment in the corporate communications and public relations fields indicates that compensation levels will continue to increase, even outpacing inflation. The hottest industry appears to be high technology, followed closely by health care. The consumer product or industrial-based business-to-business trade fields seem to be slowing down, and those recruiting PR professionals show less interest in those whose experience is in the nonprofit sector, unless the position is one with a nonprofit organization.

For More Information

This professional Canadian association for public relations professionals, with 17 member societies and 1,700 members, offers an accreditation program and opportunities for professional development.

Canadian Public Relations Society, Inc.
#720, 220 Laurier Avenue West
Ottawa, ON K1P 5Z9 Canada
Tel: 613-232-1222
Email: cprs@netcom.ca
Web: http://www.cprs.ca

The following association provides products, services, and activities for professionals in the public relations, employee communications, marketing communications, and public affairs industries. It publishes Communications Worldmagazine, holds an annual conference, and provides other resource materials. It has 12,500 members in 52 countries.

International Association of Business Communicators
One Halladie Plaza, Suite 600
San Francisco, CA 94102
Tel: 800-776-4222
Email: service centre@iabc.com
Web: http://www.iabc.com

To subscribe to this weekly newsletter for PR professionals, contact:

PR Reporter
PR Publishing Company, Inc.
PO Box 600
Exeter, NH 03833
Tel: 603-778-0514
Email: prr@prpublishing.com
Web: www.prpublishing.com

The world's largest organization for PR professionals (18,000 members, 109 chapters nationwide) provides a forum for addressing relevant issues, plus opportunities for professional development, including seminars, publications, and a national conference.

Public Relations Society of America
Career Information
33 Irving Place
New York, NY 10003
Tel: 212-995-2230
Email: hq@prsa.org
Web: http://www.prsa.org

Radio and Television Newscasters, Reporters, and Announcers

English Speech	School Subjects
Communication/ideas	Personal Skills
Primarily indoors Primarily one location	Work Environment
Some postsecondary training	Minimum Education Level
$8,000 to $23,000 to $85,000+	Salary Range
None available	Certification or Licensing
Decline	Outlook

Overview

Radio and television announcers present news and commercial messages from a script. They identify the station, announce station breaks, and introduce and close shows. Interviewing guests, making public service announcements, and conducting panel discussions may also be part of the announcer's work. In small stations the local announcer may keep the program log, run the transmitter, and cue the changeover to network broadcasting as well as write scripts or rewrite news releases. About 52,000 people are employed as radio and television announcers and newscasters in the United States.

History

Guglielmo Marconi, a young Italian engineer, first transmitted a radio signal in his home in 1895. Radio developed rapidly as people began to comprehend the tremendous possibilities. The stations KDKA in Pittsburgh and WWWJ in Detroit began broadcasting in 1920. Within 10 years, there were radio stations in all the major cities in the United States and broadcasting had become big business. The National Broadcasting Company became the first network in 1926 when it linked together 25 stations across the country. The Columbia Broadcasting System was organized in the following year. In 1934, the Mutual Broadcasting Company was founded. The years between 1930 and 1950 may be considered the zenith years of the radio industry. With the coming of television, radio broadcasting took second place in importance as entertainment for the home—but radio's commercial and communications value should not be underestimated.

Discoveries that led to the development of television can be traced as far back as 1878, when William Crookes invented a tube that produced the cathode ray. Other inventors who contributed to the development of television were Vladimir Zworykin, a Russian-born scientist who came to this country at the age of 20 and is credited with inventing the iconoscope before he was 30; Charles Jenkins, who invented a scanning disk, using certain vacuum tubes and photoelectric cells; and Philo Farnsworth, who invented an image dissector. WNBT and WCBW, the first commercially licensed television stations, went on the air in 1941 in New York. Both suspended operations during World War II but resumed them in 1946 when television sets began to be manufactured on a commercial scale.

As radio broadcasting was growing across the country in its early days, the need for announcers grew. They identified the station and brought continuity to broadcast time by linking one program with the next as well as participating in many programs. In the early days (and even today in smaller stations) announcers performed a variety of jobs around the station. When television began, many radio announcers and newscasters started to work in the new medium. The need for men and women in radio and television broadcasting has continued to grow. Television news broadcasting requires specialized "on-camera" personnel—anchors, television news reporters, broadcast news analysts, consumer reporters, and sports reporters (sportscasters).

The Job

Some announcers merely announce; others do a multitude of other jobs, depending on the size of the station. But the nature of their announcing work remains the same.

An announcer is engaged in an exacting career. The necessity for finishing a sentence or a program at a precisely planned moment makes this a demanding and often tense career. It is absolutely essential that announcers project a sense of calm to their audiences, regardless of the activity and tension behind the scenes.

The announcer who plays recorded music interspersed with a variety of advertising material and informal commentary is called a disc jockey. This title arose when most music was recorded on conventional flat records or discs. Today much of the recorded music used in commercial radio stations is on magnetic tape or compact discs. *Disc jockeys* serve as a bridge between the music itself and the listener. They may perform such public services as announcing the time, the weather forecast, or important news. It can be a lonely job, since many disc jockeys are the only person in the studio. But because their job is to maintain the good spirits of their audience and to attract new listeners, disc jockeys must possess the ability be relaxed and cheerful.

Unlike the more conventional radio or television announcer, the disc jockey is not bound by a written script. Except for the commercial announcements, which must be read as written, the disc jockey's statements are usually spontaneous. Disc jockeys usually are not required to play a musical selection to the end; they may fade out a record when it interferes with a predetermined schedule for commercials, news, time checks, or weather reports.

Announcers who cover sports events for the benefit of the listening or viewing audience are known as *sportscasters*. This is a highly specialized form of announcing as sportscasters must have extensive knowledge of the sports that they are covering, plus the ability to describe events quickly and accurately.

Often the sportscaster will spend several days with team members, observing practice sessions, interviewing people, and researching the history of an event or of the teams to be covered. The more information that a sportscaster can acquire about individual team members, company they represent, tradition of the contest, ratings of the team, and community in which the event takes place, the more interesting the coverage is to the audience.

The announcer who specializes in reporting the news to the listening or viewing public is called a *newscaster*. This job may require simply reporting facts, or it may include editorial commentary. Newscasters may be given the authority by their employers to express their opinions on news items or the philosophies of others. They must make judgments about which news is important and which is not. In some instances, they write their own scripts, based on facts that are furnished by international news bureaus. In other instances, they read text exactly as it comes in over a teletype machine. They may make as few as one or two reports each day if they work on a major news program, or they may broadcast news for five minutes every hour or half-hour. Their delivery is usually dignified, measured, and impersonal.

The *anchor* generally summarizes and comments on one aspect of the news at the end of the scheduled broadcast. This kind of announcing differs noticeably from that practiced by the sportscaster, whose manner may be breezy and interspersed with slang, or from the disc jockey, who may project a humorous, casual, or intimate image.

The newscaster may specialize in certain aspects of the news, such as economics, politics, or military activity. Newscasters also introduce films and interviews prepared by news reporters that provide in-depth coverage and information on the event being reported. Radio and television broadcasting news analysts are often called *commentators,* and they interpret specific events and discuss how these may affect individuals or the nation. They may have a specified daily slot for which material must be written, recorded, or presented live. They gather information that is analyzed and interpreted through research and interviews and cover public functions such as political conventions, press conferences, and social events.

Smaller television stations may have an announcer who performs all the functions of reporting, presenting, and commenting on the news as well as introducing network and news service reports.

Many television and radio announcers have become well-known public personalities in broadcasting. They may participate in community activities as master of ceremonies at banquets and other public events.

Requirements

Although there are no formal educational requirements for entering the field of radio and television announcing, many large stations prefer college-educated applicants. The general reason given for this preference is that announcers with broad educational and cultural backgrounds are better prepared to successfully meet a variety of unexpected or emergency situations. The greater the knowledge of geography, history, literature, the arts, political science, music, science, and of the sound and structure of the English language, the greater the announcer's value.

High School

In high school, you should focus on a college preparatory curriculum, according to Steve Bell, a professor of telecommunications at Ball State University. A former network anchor who now teaches broadcast journalism, he says, "One trend that concerns me is that some high schools are developing elaborate radio and television journalism programs that take up large chunks of academic time, and I think that is getting the cart before the horse. There's nothing wrong with one broadcast journalism course or extracurricular activities, but not at the expense of academic hours."

In that college preparatory curriculum, you should learn how to write and use the English language in literature and communication classes. Subjects such as history, government, economics, and a foreign language are also important.

Postsecondary Training

When it comes to college, having your focus in the right place is essential, according to Professor Bell. "You want to be sure you're going to a college or university that has a strong program in broadcast journalism, where they also put a strong emphasis on the liberal arts core."

Some advocate a more vocational type of training in preparation for broadcast journalism, but Bell cautions against strictly vocational training. "The ultimate purpose of college is to have more of an education than you have from a trade school. It is important to obtain a broad-based understanding of the world we live in, especially if your career goal is to become an anchor."

A strong liberal arts background with emphasis in journalism, English, political science, or economics is advised, as well as a telecommunications or communications major.

Other Requirements

A pleasing voice and personality are of great importance to prospective announcers. They must be levelheaded and able to react calmly in the face of a major crisis. People's lives may depend on an announcer's ability to remain calm during a disaster. There are also many unexpected circumstances that demand the skill of quick thinking. For example, if guests who are to appear on a program do not arrive or become too nervous to go on the air, the announcer must compensate immediately and fill the airtime. He or she must smooth over an awkward phrase, breakdown in equipment, or other technical difficulty.

Good diction and English usage, thorough knowledge of correct pronunciation, and freedom from regional dialects are very important. A factual error, grammatical error, or mispronounced word can bring letters of criticism to station managers.

Those who aspire to careers as television announcers must present a good appearance and have no nervous mannerisms. Neatness, cleanliness, and careful attention to the details of proper dress are important. The successful television announcer must have the combination of sincerity and showmanship that attracts and captures an audience.

Broadcast announcing is a highly competitive field. Although there may not be any specific training program required by prospective employers, station officials pay particular attention to taped auditions of an applicant's delivery or, in the case of television, to videotaped demos of sample presentations.

A Federal Communications Commission license or permit is no longer required for broadcasting positions. Union membership may be required for employment with large stations in major cities and is a necessity with the networks. The largest talent union is the American Federation of Television and Radio Artists (AFTRA). Most small stations, however, are nonunion.

Exploring

If a career as an announcer sounds interesting, try to get a summer job at a radio or television station. Although you will probably not have the opportunity to broadcast, you may be able to judge whether or not the type of work appeals to you as a career.

Any chance to speak or perform before an audience should be welcomed. Appearing as a speaker or performer can show whether or not you have the stage presence necessary for a career in front of a microphone or camera.

Many colleges and universities have their own radio and television stations and offer courses in radio and television. You can gain valuable experience working at college-owned stations. Some radio stations, cable systems, and TV stations offer financial assistance, internships, and co-op work programs, as well as scholarships and fellowships.

Employers

Almost all radio and television announcers are on staff at one of the 12,199 radio stations or 1,580 television stations around the country. Some, however, work on a freelance basis on individual assignments for networks, stations, advertising agencies, and other producers of commercials.

Some companies own several television or radio stations; some belong to networks such as ABC, CBS, NBC, or FOX, while others are independent. While radio and television stations are located throughout the United States, major markets, where better paying jobs are found, are generally near large metropolitan areas.

Starting Out

One way to enter this field is to apply for an entry-level job rather than an announcer position. It is also advisable to start at a small station. Most announcers start in jobs such as production secretary, production assistant, researcher, or reporter in small stations. As opportunities arise, they move from one job to another. Work as a disc jockey, sportscaster, or news reporter may become available. Network jobs are few, and the competition for them is great. An announcer must have several years of experience as well as a college education to be considered for these positions.

An announcer is employed only after an audition. Applicants should carefully select audition material to show a prospective employer the full range of one's abilities. In addition to presenting prepared materials, applicants may be asked to read material that they have not seen previously, such as a commercial, news release, dramatic selection, or poem.

Advancement

Most successful announcers advance from small stations to large ones. Experienced announcers usually have held several jobs. The most successful announcers may be those who work for the networks. Usually, because of network locations, announcers must live in or near the country's largest cities.

Some careers lead from announcing to other aspects of radio or television work. More people are employed in sales, promotion, and planning than in performing; often they are paid more than announcers. Because the networks employ relatively few announcers in proportion to the rest of the broadcasting professionals, a candidate must have several years of experience and specific background in several news areas before being considered for an audition. These top announcers generally are college graduates.

Earnings

According to a 1998 Salary Survey by the Radio and Television News Directors Association (RTNDA), there is a wide range of salaries for announcers. For radio reporters and announcers, the median salary was $20,000 with a low of $10,000 and a high of $75,000. For television reporters and announcers, the median salary was $23,000 with a low of $8,000 and a high of $85,000.

For both radio and television, salaries are higher in the larger markets. Nationally known announcers and newscasters who appear regularly on network television programs receive salaries that may be quite impressive. For those who become top television personalities in large metropolitan areas, salaries also are quite rewarding.

Most radio or television stations broadcast 24 hours a day. Although much of the material may be prerecorded, announcing staff must often be available and as a result may work considerable overtime or split shifts, especially in smaller stations. Evening, night, weekend, and holiday duty may provide additional compensation.

Work Environment

Work in radio and television stations is usually very pleasant. Almost all stations are housed in modern facilities. The maintenance of technical electronic equipment requires temperature and dust control, and people who work around such equipment benefit from the precautions taken to preserve it.

Announcers' jobs may provide opportunities to meet well-known or celebrity persons. Being at the center of an important communications medium can make the broadcaster more keenly aware of current issues and divergent points of view than the average person.

Announcers and newscasters usually work a 40-hour week, but they may work irregular hours. They may report for work at a very early hour in the morning or work late into the night. Some radio stations operate on a 24-hour basis. All-night announcers may be alone in the station during their working hours.

Outlook

About 52,000 people are employed as radio and television announcers and newscasters in the United States. Competition for entry-level employment in announcing during the coming years is expected to be keen as the broadcasting industry always attracts more applicants than are needed to fill available openings. There is a better chance of working in radio than in television because there are more radio stations. Local television stations usually carry a high percentage of network programs and need only a very small staff to carry out local operations.

The U.S. Department of Labor predicts that opportunities for experienced broadcasting personnel will decrease through the year 2006 due to the lack of growth in the number of new radio and television stations. Openings will result mainly from those who leave the industry or the labor force. The trend among major networks, and to some extent among many smaller radio and TV stations, is toward specialization in such fields as sportscasting or weather forecasting. Newscasters who specialize in such areas as business, consumer, and health news should have an advantage over other job applicants.

For More Information

For information on its summer internship program, contact:

The Association of Local Television Stations
1320 19th Street, NW, Suite 300
Washington, DC 20036
Tel: 202-887-1970
Email: info@altv.com
Web: http://www.altv.com

For a list of schools offering degrees in broadcasting, write to:

Broadcast Education Association
1771 N Street, NW
Washington, DC 20036-2891
Tel: 202-429-5354
Email: fweaber@nab.org
Web: http://www.beaweb.org

For broadcast education, support, and scholarship information, contact:

National Association of Broadcasters
1771 N Street, NW
Washington, DC 20036-2891
Tel: 202-429-5300
Web: http://www.nab.org

For college programs and union information, contact:

National Association of Broadcast Employees and Technicians
501 3rd Street, NW, 8th Floor
Washington, DC 20001
Tel: 202-434-1254
Email: nabet@nabetcwa.org
Web: http://nabetcwa.org

For general information, contact:

National Association of Farm Broadcasters
26 East Exchange Street, Suite 307
St. Paul, MN 55101
Tel: 612-224-0508
Email: nafboffice@aol.com
Web: http://nafb.com

For scholarship and internship information, contact:

Radio-Television News Directors Association
Radio-Television News Directors Foundation
1000 Connecticut Avenue, NW, Suite 615
Washington, DC 20036-5302
Tel: 202-659-6510
Email: rtnda@rtnda.org
Web: http://www.rtnda.org

Reporters

English Journalism	School Subjects
Communication/ideas Helping/teaching	Personal Skills
Indoors and outdoors Primarily multiple locations	Work Environment
Bachelor's degree	Minimum Education Level
$25,000 to $50,000 to $100,000+	Salary Range
None available	Certification or Licensing
Little change or more slowly than the average	Outlook

Overview

Reporters are the foot soldiers for newspapers, magazines, and television and radio broadcast companies. They gather and analyze information about current events and write stories for publication or for broadcasting.

History

Newspapers are primary disseminators of news in the United States. People read newspapers to learn about the current events that are shaping their society and societies around the world. Newspapers give public expression to opinion and criticism of government and societal issues, and of course, provide the public with entertaining, informative reading.

Newspapers are able to fulfill these functions because of the freedom given to the press. However, this was not always the case. The first American newspaper, published in 1690, was suppressed four days after it was published. And it was not until 1704 that the first continuous newspaper appeared.

One early newspaperman who later became a famous writer was Benjamin Franklin. Franklin worked for his brother at a Boston newspaper before publishing his own two years later in 1723 in Philadelphia.

A number of developments in the printing industry made it possible for newspapers to be printed more cheaply. In the late 19th century, new types of presses were developed to increase production, and more important, the linotype machine was invented. The linotype mechanically set the letters so that handset type was no longer necessary. This dramatically decreased the amount of prepress time needed to get a page into print. Newspapers could respond to breaking stories more quickly; late editions with breaking stories became part of the news world.

These technological advances, along with an increasing population, factored in the rapid growth of the newspaper industry in the United States. In 1776, there were only 37 newspapers in the United States. Today there are more than 1,500 daily and nearly 7,500 weekly newspapers in the country.

As newspapers grew in size and widened the scope of their coverage, it became necessary to increase the number of employees and to assign them specialized jobs. Reporters have always been the heart of newspaper staffs. However, in today's complex world, with the public hungry for news as it occurs, reporters and correspondents are involved in all media—not only newspapers, but magazines, radio, and television as well. Today, with the advent of the Internet, many newspapers are going online, causing many reporters to become active participants on the information superhighway.

The Job

Reporters collect information on newsworthy events and prepare stories for newspaper or magazine publication or for radio or television broadcast. The stories may simply provide information about local, state, or national events, or they may present opposing points of view on issues of current interest. In this latter capacity, the press plays an important role in monitoring the actions of public officials and others in positions of power.

Stories may originate as an assignment from an editor or as the result of a lead or news tip. Good reporters are always on the lookout for good story ideas. To cover a story, they gather and verify facts by interviewing people involved in or related to the event, examining documents and public records, observing events as they happen, and researching relevant background information. Reporters generally take notes or use a tape recorder as they collect information and write their stories once they return to their offices. In order to meet a deadline, they may have to telephone the stories to rewriters, who write or transcribe the stories for them. After the facts have been gathered and verified, the reporters transcribe their notes, organize their material, and determine what emphasis, or angle, to give the news. The story is then written to meet prescribed standards of editorial style and format.

The basic functions of reporters are to observe events objectively and impartially, record them accurately, and explain what the news means in a larger, societal context. Within this framework, there are several types of reporters.

The most basic is the *news reporter*. This job sometimes involves covering a beat, such as the police station, courthouse, or school system. It may involve receiving general assignments, such as a story about an unusual occurrence or an obituary of a community leader. Large daily papers may assign teams of reporters to investigate social, economic, or political events and conditions.

Many newspaper, wire service, and magazine reporters specialize in one type of story, either because they have a particular interest in the subject or because they have acquired the expertise to analyze and interpret news in that particular area. Topical reporters cover stories for a specific department, such as medicine, politics, foreign affairs, sports, consumer affairs, finance, science, business, education, labor, or religion. They sometimes write features explaining the history that has led up to certain events in the field they cover. *Feature writers* generally write longer, broader stories than news reporters, usually on more upbeat subjects, such as fashion, art, theater, travel, and social events. They may write about trends, for example, or profile local celebrities. *Editorial writers* and *syndicated news columnists* present viewpoints that, although based on a thorough knowledge, are opinions on topics of popular interest. *Columnists* write under a byline and usually specialize in a particular subject, such as politics or government activities. *Critics* review restaurants, books, works of art, movies, plays, musical performances, and other cultural events.

Specializing allows reporters to focus their efforts, talent, and knowledge on one area of expertise. It also allows them more opportunities to develop deeper relationships with contacts and sources necessary to gain access to the news.

Correspondents report events in locations distant from their home offices. They may report news by mail, telephone, fax, or computer from rural areas, large cities throughout the United States, or countries. Many large newspapers, magazines, and broadcast companies have one correspondent who is responsible for covering all the news for the foreign city or country where they are based.

Reporters on small or weekly newspapers not only cover all aspects of the news in their communities, but they also may take photographs, write editorials and headlines, lay out pages, edit wire-service copy, and help with general office work. *Television reporters* may have to be photogenic as well as talented and resourceful. They may at times present live reports, filmed by a mobile camera unit at the scene where the news originates, or they may tape interviews and narration for later broadcast.

Requirements

High School

High school courses that provide a firm foundation for a career as reporter include English, journalism, social studies, speech, typing, and computer science.

Postsecondary Training

A bachelor's degree is essential for aspiring reporters. Graduate degrees give students a great advantage over those entering the field with lesser degrees. Most editors prefer applicants with degrees in journalism because their studies include liberal arts courses as well as professional training in journalism. Some editors consider it sufficient for a reporter to have a good general education from a liberal arts college. Others prefer applicants with an undergraduate degree in liberal arts and a master's degree in journalism. The great majority of journalism graduates hired today by newspapers, wire services, and magazines have majored specifically in news-editorial journalism.

More than 400 colleges offer programs in journalism leading to a bachelor's degree. In these schools, around three-fourths of a student's time is devoted to a liberal education and one-fourth to the professional study of journalism, with required courses such as introductory mass media, basic reporting and copy editing, history of journalism, and press law and ethics. Students are encouraged to select other journalism courses according to their specific interests.

Journalism courses and programs are also offered by more than 350 community and junior colleges. Graduates of these programs are prepared to go to work directly as general assignment reporters, but they may encounter difficulty when competing with graduates of four-year programs. Credit earned in community and junior colleges may be transferable to four-year programs in journalism at other colleges and universities. Journalism training may also be obtained in the armed forces. Names and addresses of newspapers and a list of journalism schools and departments are published in the *Editor and Publisher International Year Book,* which is available for reference in most public libraries and newspaper offices.

A master's degree in journalism may be earned at more than 100 schools, and a doctorate at about 20 schools. Graduate degrees may prepare students specifically for careers in news or as journalism teachers, researchers, and theorists or for jobs in advertising or public relations.

A reporter's liberal arts training should include courses in English (with an emphasis on writing), sociology, political science, economics, history, psychology, business, speech, and computer science. Knowledge of foreign languages is also useful. To be a reporter in a specialized field, such as science or finance, requires concentrated course work in that area.

Other Requirements

A crucial requirement for reporters is typing skill. Reporters type their stories using word processing programs. Although not essential, a knowledge of shorthand or speedwriting makes note taking easier, and an acquaintance with news photography is an asset.

Reporters must be inquisitive, aggressive, persistent, and detail-oriented. They must enjoy interaction with people of various races, cultures, religions, economic levels, and social statuses.

Exploring

You can explore a career as a reporter in a number of ways. You can talk to reporters and editors at local newspapers and radio and TV stations. You can interview the admissions counselor at the school of journalism closest to your home.

In addition to taking courses in English, journalism, social studies, speech, computer science, and typing, high school students can acquire practical experience by working on school newspapers or on a church, synagogue, or mosque newsletter. Part-time and summer jobs on newspapers provide invaluable experience to the aspiring reporter.

College students can develop their reporting skills in the laboratory courses or workshops that are part of the journalism curriculum. College students might also accept jobs as campus correspondents for selected newspapers. People who work as part-time reporters covering news in a particular area of a community are known as stringers and are paid only for those stories that are printed.

More than 3,000 journalism scholarships, fellowships, and assistantships are offered by universities, newspapers, foundations, and professional organizations to college students. Many newspapers and magazines offer summer internships to journalism students to provide them with practical experience in a variety of basic reporting and editing duties. Students who successfully complete internships are usually placed in jobs more quickly upon graduation than those without such experience.

Employers

Of the approximately 60,000 reporters and correspondents employed in the late 1990s, about 63 percent worked for newspapers of all sizes. The rest were employed by wire services, magazines, and radio and television broadcasting companies.

Starting Out

Jobs in this field may be obtained through college placement offices or by applying directly to the personnel departments of individual employers. Applicants with some practical experience will have an advantage; they should be prepared to present a portfolio of material they wrote as volunteer or part-time reporters or other writing samples.

Most journalism school graduates start out as general assignment reporters or copy editors for small publications. A few outstanding journalism graduates may be hired by large city newspapers or national magazines. They are trained on the job. But they are the exception, as large employers usually require several years' experience. As a rule, novice reporters cover routine assignments, such as reporting on civic and club meetings, writing obituaries, or summarizing speeches. As reporters become more skilled, they are assigned to more important events or to a regular beat, or they may specialize in a particular field.

Advancement

Reporters may advance by moving to larger newspapers or press services, but competition for such positions is unusually keen. Many highly qualified reporters apply for these jobs every year.

A select number of reporters eventually become columnists, correspondents, editorial writers, editors, or top executives. These important and influential positions represent the top of the field, and competition is strong for them.

Many reporters transfer the contacts and knowledge developed in newspaper reporting to related fields, such as public relations, advertising, or preparing copy for radio and television news programs.

Earnings

There are great variations in the earnings of reporters. Salaries are related to experience, kind of employer for which the reporter works, geographical location, and whether the reporter is covered by a contract negotiated by the Newspaper Guild.

In the late 1990s, reporters on daily newspapers having Newspaper Guild contracts receive starting salaries that ranged from about $10,000 in Battle Creek, Michigan, to $68,000 in New York City. The average starting salary was about $25,000. Reporters with between two and six years of experience earned salaries that ranged from $18,000 to $70,000. Some top reporters on big city dailies earned even more, on the basis of merit or seniority.

Reporters who worked for radio earned an average salary of $15,000 a year. Some who worked for stations in large cities earned up to $36,000. Reporters who worked in television earned between $17,000 and $75,000, depending on the size of the station. High-profile columnists and newscasters working for prestigious papers or network television stations earned over $100,000 a year.

Work Environment

Reporters work under a great deal of pressure in settings that differ from the typical business office. Their jobs generally require a five-day, 35- to 40-hour week, but overtime and irregular schedules are very common. Reporters employed by morning papers start work in the late afternoon and finish around midnight, while those on afternoon or evening papers start early in the morning and work until early or midafternoon. Foreign correspondents often work late at night to send the news to their papers in time to meet printing deadlines.

The day of the smoky, ink-stained newsroom has passed, but newspaper offices are still hectic places. Reporters have to work amid the clatter of computer keyboards and other machines, loud voices engaged in telephone conversations, and the bustle created by people hurrying about. An atmosphere of excitement and bustle prevails, especially as press deadlines approach.

Travel is often required in this occupation, and some assignments may be dangerous, such as covering wars, political uprisings, fires, floods, and other events of a volatile nature.

Outlook

The employment outlook for reporters and correspondents through 2006 is expected to grow somewhat slower than the average for all occupations. According to the Bureau of Labor Statistics projections, the number of employed reporters and correspondents is projected to decline by about 3 percent within the next several years. While the number of self-employed reporters and correspondents is expected to grow about 9 percent by 2006, and magazine workers by about 7 percent, newpaper jobs are expected to decrease by about 9 percent, and jobs in other communications settings also are projected to decline slightly.

Because of an increase in the number of small community and suburban daily and weekly newspapers, opportunities will be best for journalism graduates who are willing to relocate and accept relatively low starting salaries. With experience, reporters on these small papers can move up to editing positions or may choose to transfer to reporting jobs on larger newspapers or magazines.

Openings will be limited on big city dailies. While individual papers may enlarge their reporting staffs, little or no change is expected in the total number of these newspapers. Applicants will face strong competition for jobs on large metropolitan newspapers. Experience is a definite requirement, which rules out most new graduates unless they possess credentials in an area for which the publication has a pressing need. Occasionally, a beginner can use contacts and experience gained through internship programs and summer jobs to obtain a reporting job immediately after graduation.

A significant number of jobs will be provided by magazines and in radio and television broadcasting, but the major news magazines and larger broadcasting stations generally prefer experienced reporters. For beginning correspondents, small stations with local news broadcasts will continue to replace staff who move on to larger stations or leave the business. Network hiring has been cut drastically in the past few years and will probably continue to decline.

Overall, the prospects are best for graduates who have majored in news-editorial journalism and completed an internship while in school. The top graduates in an accredited program will have a great advantage, as will talented technical or scientific writers. Small newspapers prefer to hire beginning reporters who are acquainted with the community and are willing to help with photography and other aspects of production. Without at least a bachelor's degree in journalism, applicants will find it increasingly difficult to obtain even an entry-level position.

Those with doctorates and practical reporting experience may find teaching positions at four-year colleges and universities, while highly qualified reporters with master's degrees may obtain employment in journalism departments of community and junior colleges.

Poor economic conditions do not drastically affect the employment of reporters and correspondents. Their numbers are not severely cut back even during a downturn; instead, employers forced to reduce expenditures will suspend new hiring.

For More Information

This organization provides general educational information on all areas of journalism (newspapers, magazines, television, and radio). A Look at Careers in Journalism and Mass Communications, *12 pages, describes the various career opportunities in the field.*

Association for Education in Journalism and Mass Communication
University of South Carolina
1621 College Street
Columbia, SC 29208
Tel: 803-777-2006

To receive a copy of The Journalist's Road to Success, *which lists schools offering degrees in news-editorial and financial aid to those interested in print journalism, contact:*

Dow Jones Newspaper Fund
PO Box 300
Princeton, NJ 08543-0300
Tel: 609-452-2820
Email: newsfund@plink.geis.com
Web: http://www.dj.com/newsfund

To receive a free copy of Newspaper: What's in It for Me? *write:*

Newspaper Careers Project
Fulfillment Department NAA Foundation
11600 Sunrise Valley Drive
Reston, VA 22091

Screenwriters

School Subjects
English
Theater/Dance

Personal Skills
Artistic
Communication/ideas

Work Environment
Primarily indoors
Primarily one location

Minimum Education Level
High school diploma

Salary Range
$15,000 to $83,542 to $500,000+

Certification or Licensing
None available

Outlook
Faster than the average

Overview

Screenwriters write scripts for entertainment, education, training, sales, and films. They may choose themes themselves, or they may write on a theme assigned by a producer or director, sometimes adapting plays or novels into screenplays. Screenwriting is an art, a craft, and a business. It is a career that requires imagination and creativity, the ability to tell a story using both dialogue and pictures, and the ability to negotiate with producers and studio executives.

History

In 1894, Thomas Edison invented the kinetograph to take a series of pictures of actions staged specifically for the camera. In October of the same year, the first film opened at Hoyt's Theatre in New York. It was a series of acts performed by such characters as a strongman, a contortionist, and trained animals. Even in these earliest motion pictures, the plot or sequence of actions the film would portray was written down before filming began.

Newspaperman Roy McCardell was the first person to be hired for the specific job of writing for motion pictures. He wrote captions for photographs in an entertainment weekly. When he was employed by Biograph to write 10 scenarios, or stories, at $10 apiece, it caused a flood of newspapermen to try their hand at screenwriting.

The early films, which ran only about a minute and were photographs of interesting movement, grew into story films, which ran between 9 and 15 minutes. The demand for original plots led to the development of story departments at each of the motion picture companies in the period from 1910 to 1915. The story departments were responsible for writing the stories and also for reading and evaluating material that came from outside sources. Stories usually came from writers, but some were purchased from actors on the lot. The actor Genevieve (Gene) Gauntier, was paid $20 per reel of film for her first scenarios.

There was a continuing need for scripts because usually a studio bought a story one month, filmed the next, and released the film the month after. Some of the most popular stories in these early films were Wild West tales and comedies.

Longer story films began to use titles, and as motion pictures became longer and more sophisticated, so did the titles. In 1909-10, there was an average of 80 feet of title per 1,000 feet of film. By 1926, the average increased to 250 feet of title per 1,000 feet. The titles included dialogue, description, and historical background.

In 1920, the first Screen Writers Guild was established to ensure fair treatment of writers, and in 1927 the Academy of Motion Picture Arts and Sciences was formed, including a branch for writers. The first sound film, *The Jazz Singer,* was also produced in 1927. Screenwriting changed dramatically to adapt to the new technology.

From the 1950s to the 1980s, the studios gradually declined and more independent film companies and individuals were able to break into the motion picture industry. The television industry began to thrive in the 1950s, further increasing the number of opportunities for screenwriters. During the 1960s, people began to graduate from the first education programs developed specifically for screenwriting.

Today, most Americans have spent countless hours viewing programs on television and movie screens. Familiarity with these mediums has led many writers to attempt writing screenplays. This has created an intensely fierce marketplace with many more screenplays being rejected than accepted each year.

The Job

Screenwriters write dramas, comedies, soap operas, adventures, westerns, documentaries, newscasts, and training films. They may write original stories, or get inspiration from newspapers, magazines, or books. They may also write scripts for continuing television series. Continuity writers in broadcasting create station announcements, previews of coming shows, and advertising copy for local sponsors. Broadcasting scriptwriters usually work in a team, writing for a certain audience, to fill a certain time slot. Motion picture writers submit an original screenplay or adaptation of a book to a motion picture producer or studio. Playwrights submit their plays to drama companies for performance or try to get their work published in book form.

Screenwriters may work on a staff of writers and producers for a large company. Or they may work independently for smaller companies which hire only freelance production teams. Advertising agencies also hire writers, sometimes as staff, sometimes as freelancers.

Scripts are written in a 2-column format, 1 column for dialogue and sound, the other for video instructions. One page of script equals about 1 minute of running time, though it varies. Each page has about 150 words and takes about 20 seconds to read. Screenwriters send a query letter outlining their idea before they submit a script to a production company. Then they send a standard release form and wait at least a month for a response. Studios buy many more scripts than are actually produced, and studios often will buy a script only with provisions that the original writer or another writer will rewrite it to their specifications.

Requirements

High School

You can develop your writing skills in English, theater, speech, and journalism classes. Belonging to a debate team can also help you learn how to express your ideas within a specific time allotment and framework. History, government, and foreign language can contribute to a well-rounded education, necessary for creating intelligent scripts. A business course can be useful in understanding the complex nature of the film industry.

Postsecondary Training

There are no set educational requirements for screenwriters. A college degree is desirable, especially a liberal arts education which exposes you to a wide range of subjects. An undergraduate or graduate film program will likely include courses in screenwriting, film theory, and other subjects that will teach you about the film industry and its history. A creative writing program will involve you with workshops and seminars that will help you develop fiction writing skills.

Other Requirements

As a screenwriter, you must be able to create believable characters and develop a story. You must have technical skills, such as dialogue writing, creating plots, and doing research. In addition to creativity and originality, you also need an understanding of the marketplace for your work—you should be aware of what kinds of scripts are in demand by producers. Word processing skills are also helpful.

Exploring

One of the best ways to learn about screenwriting is to read and study scripts. It is advisable to watch a motion picture while simultaneously following the script. The scripts for such classic films as *Casablanca*, *Network*, and *Chinatown* are often taught in college screenwriting courses. You should read film-industry publications, such as *Daily Variety*, *Hollywood Reporter*, and *The Hollywood Scriptwriter*. There are a number of books about screenwriting, but they're often written by those outside of the industry. These books are best used primarily for learning about the format required for writing a screenplay. There are also computer software programs which assist with screenplay formatting.

The Sundance Institute, a Utah-based production company, accepts unsolicited scripts from those who have read the institute's submission guidelines. Every January they choose a few scripts and invite the writers to a five-day program of one-on-one sessions with professionals. The process is repeated in June, and also includes a videotaping of sections of chosen scripts. The Institute doesn't produce features, but they can often introduce writers to those who do. (For guidelines, send a self-addressed, stamped envelope with your request to The Sundance Institute, 225 Santa Monica

Boulevard, 8th Floor, Santa Monica, CA 90401, or visit their Web site at http://www.sundance.org.)

Most states offer grants for emerging and established screenwriters and other artists. Contact your state's arts council for guidelines and application materials. In addition, several arts groups and associations hold annual contests for screenwriters. To find out more about screenwriting contests, consult a reference work such as *The Writer's Market*.

Students may try to get their work performed locally. A teacher may be able to help you submit your work to a local radio or television station or to a publisher of plays.

Employers

Most screenwriters work on a freelance basis, contracting with production companies for individual projects. Those who work for television may contract with a TV production company for a certain number of episodes or seasons.

Starting Out

The first step to getting a screenplay produced is to write a letter to the script editor of a production company describing yourself, your training, and your work. Ask if the editors would be interested in reading one of your scripts. You should also pursue a manager or agent by sending along a brief letter describing a project you're working on. (A list of agents is available from the Writers Guild of America (WGA).) If you receive an invitation to submit more, you'll then prepare a synopsis or treatment of the screenplay, which is usually from 1 to 10 pages. It should be in the form of a narrative short story, with little or no dialogue.

Whether you are a beginning or experienced screenwriter, it is best to have an agent, since studios, producers and stars often return unsolicited manuscripts unopened to protect themselves from plagiarism charges. Agents provide access to studios and producers, interpret contracts, and negotiate deals.

It is wise to register your script ($10 for members, $20 for nonmembers) with the WGA. Although registration offers no legal protection, it is proof that on a specific date you came up with a particular idea, treatment, or script. You should also keep a detailed journal that lists the contacts you've made, the people who have read your script, etc.

Advancement

Competition is stiff among screenwriters, and a beginner will find it difficult to break into the field. More opportunities become available as you gain experience and a reputation, but that is a process that can take many years. Rejection is a common occurrence in the field of screenwriting. Most successful screenwriters have had to send their screenplays to numerous production companies before they find one who likes their work.

Once you've sold some scripts, you may be able to join the WGA. Membership with the WGA guarantees you a minimum wage for a production and other benefits such as arbitration. Some screenwriters, however, writing for minor productions, can have regular work and successful careers without WGA membership.

Those screenwriters who manage to break into the business can benefit greatly from recognition in the industry. In addition to creating their own scripts, some writers are also hired to "doctor" the scripts of others, using their expertise to revise scripts for production. If a film proves very successful, a screenwriter will be able to command higher payment, and will be able to work on high-profile productions. Some of the most talented screenwriters receive awards from the industry, most notably the Academy Award for best original or adapted screenplay.

Earnings

Wages for screenwriters are nearly impossible to track. Some screenwriters make hundreds of thousands of dollars from their scripts, while others write and film their own scripts without any payment at all, relying on backers and loans. Screenwriter Joe Eszterhas made entertainment news in the early 1990s when he received $3 million for each of his treatments for *Basic Instinct, Jade,* and *Showgirls.* In 1999, many scripts by first-time screenwriters have been sold for between $500,000 and $1 million. Typically, a writer will earn a percentage (approximately 1 percent) of the film's budget. Obviously, a lower-budget film pays considerably less than a big production. According to statistics compiled in 1998 by the WGA, the median income for WGA members was $83,542 a year. As a member of the WGA, you can receive health benefits.

Work Environment

Screenwriters who choose to freelance have the freedom to write when and where they choose. They must be persistent and patient—only 1 in 20 to 30 purchased or optioned screenplays is produced.

Screenwriters who work on the staff of a large company, for a television series, or under contract to a motion picture company, may share writing duties with others.

Screenwriters who do not live in Hollywood or New York will likely have to travel to attend script conferences. They may even have to relocate for several weeks while a project is in production. Busy periods before and during film production are followed by long periods of inactivity and solitude. This forces many screenwriters, especially those just getting started in the field, to work other jobs and pursue other careers while they develop their talent and craft.

Outlook

There is intense competition in the television and motion picture industries. There are currently over 9,300 members of the WGA. A 1998 report by the WGA found that only 4,164 of its members were actually employed the previous year. The report also focused on the opportunities for women and minority screenwriters throughout the 1990s. Despite employment for minority screenwriters substantially increasing, employment for women changed little in that decade. Eighty percent of those writing for feature films are white males. Though this domination in the industry will eventually change because of efforts by women and minority filmmakers, the change may be slow in coming. The success of independent cinema, which has introduced a number of women and minority filmmakers to the industry, will continue to contribute to this change.

As cable television expands and digital technology allows for more programming, new opportunities may emerge. Television networks continue to need new material and new episodes for long-running series. Studios are always looking for new angles on action, adventure, horror, and comedy, especially romantic comedy stories. The demand for new screenplays should increase slightly in the next decade, but the number of screenwriters is growing at a faster rate. Writers will continue to find opportunities in advertising agencies and educational and training video production houses.

For More Information

To learn more about the film industry, to read interviews and articles by noted screenwriters, and to find links to many other screenwriting-related sites on the Internet, visit the Web sites of the WGA:

Writers Guild of America
West Chapter
7000 West Third Street
Los Angeles, CA 90048
Tel: 310-550-1000
Web: http://www.wga.org

Writers Guild of America
East Chapter
555 West 57th Street
New York, NY 10019
Tel: 212-767-7800
Web: http://www.wgaeast.org

Check out this site for a number of Web resources for screenwriters:

Screenwriters & Playwrights Home Page
Web: http://www.teleport.com/~cdeemer/scrwriter.html

Songwriters

School Subjects	English Music
Personal Skills	Artistic Communication/ideas
Work Environment	Primarily indoors Primarily one location
Minimum Education Level	High school diploma
Salary Range	$20,000 to $50,000 to $1,000,000+
Certification or Licensing	None available
Outlook	About as fast as the average

Overview

Songwriters write the words and music for songs, including songs for recordings, advertising jingles, and theatrical performances. We hear the work of songwriters every day, and yet most songwriters remain anonymous, even if a song's performer is famous. Many songwriters, of course, perform their own songs.

History

Songwriting played an important part in the growth of the United States. The early pioneers wrote songs as a way to relax. Some of the difficult experiences of traveling, fighting over land, farming, and hunting for food were put into words by early songwriters, and the words set to music, for the guitar, banjo, piano, and other instruments. Francis Scott Key (1780?-1843) became famous for writing the words to the "Star Spangled Banner," set to a popular drinking tune.

Toward the end of the 19th century, sheet music was sold by dozens and even hundreds of publishing companies, centered in New York City in what became known as Tin Pan Alley. This name was coined by a songwriter and journalist named Monroe Rosenfeld, referring to the sounds of many voices and pianos coming from the open windows of the street where many of the music publishers were located. By the 1880s, sheet music sold in the millions; most songs were introduced on the stages of musical theater, vaudeville, and burlesque shows. Radio became an important medium for introducing new songs in the 1920s, followed by the introduction of sound movies in the 1930s. Sheet music became less important as musical recordings were introduced. This presented difficulties for the songwriter and publisher, because the sales of sheet music were easier to control. In the 1940s, the first associations for protecting the rights of the songwriters and publishers were formed; among the benefits songwriters received were royalties for each time a song they had written was recorded, performed, or played on the radio or in film.

By the 1950s, Tin Pan Alley no longer referred to a specific area in New York but was used nationwide to denote popular songs in general, and especially a type of simple melody and sentimental and often silly lyric that dominated the pop music industry. The rise of rock and roll music in the 1950s put an end to Tin Pan Alley's dominance. Many performers began to write their own songs, a trend that became particularly important in the 1960s. In the late 1970s, a new type of songwriting emerged. Rap music, featuring words chanted over a musical background, seemed to bring songwriting full circle, back to the oral traditions of its origins.

The Job

There are many different ways to write a song. A song may begin with a few words—the lyric—or with a few notes of a melody, or a song may be suggested by an idea, theme, or product. A song may come about in a flash of inspiration or may be developed slowly over a long period of time. Songwriters may work alone, or as part of a team, in which one person concentrates on the lyrics while another person concentrates on the music. Sometimes there may be several people working on the same song.

"One of the most important things," says songwriter Beth McBride, "is collecting your ideas, even if they're only fragments of ideas, and writing them down. Sometimes a song comes to me from beginning to end, but I can't always rely on inspiration." Beth performed with the band "B and the Hot Notes," for which she wrote and recorded original music. She currently fronts a musical duo called "Acoustisaurus Rex" and is involved in another recording project. "A lot of my writing has been personal, derived from experience. Also from the observation of others' experiences."

Most popular songs require words, or lyrics, and some songwriters may concentrate on writing the words to a song. These songwriters are called lyricists. Events, experiences, or emotions may inspire a lyricist to write lyrics. A lyricist may also be contracted to write the words for a jingle, a musical, or adapt the words from an existing song for another project.

Some songwriters do no more than write the words to a potential song, and leave it to others to develop a melody and musical accompaniment for the words. They may sell the words to a music publisher, or work in a team to create a finished song from the lyric. Some lyricists specialize in writing the words for advertising jingles. They are usually employed by advertising agencies and may work on several different products at once, often under pressure of a deadline.

In songwriting teams, one member may be a lyricist, while the other member is a composer. The development of a song can be a highly collaborative process. The composer might suggest topics for the song to the lyricist; the lyricist might suggest a melody to the composer. Other times, the composer plays a musical piece for the lyricist, and the lyricist tries to create lyrics to fit with that piece.

Composers for popular music generally have a strong background in music, and often in performing music as well. They must have an understanding of many musical styles, so that they can develop the music that will fit a project's needs. Composers work with a variety of musical and electronic equipment, including computers, to produce and record their music. They develop the different parts for the different musical instruments needed to play the song. They also work with musicians who will play and record the song, and the composer conducts or otherwise directs the musicians as the song is played.

Songwriters, composers, and musicians often make use of MIDI (musical instrument digital interface) technology to produce sounds through synthesizers, drum machines, and samplers. These sounds are usually controlled by a computer, and the composer or songwriter can mix, alter, and refine the sounds using mixing boards and computer software. Like analog or acoustic instruments, which produce sounds as a string or reed or drum head vibrates with air, MIDI creates digital "vibrations" that can produce sounds similar to acoustic instruments or highly unusual sounds invented by the songwriter. Synthesizers and other sound-producing machines may each have their own keyboard or playing mechanism, or be linked through one or more keyboards. They may also be controlled through the computer, or with other types of controls, such as a guitar controller, which plays like a guitar, or foot controls. Songs can be stored in the computer, or transferred to tape or compact disc.

Many, if not most, songwriters combine both the work of a lyricist and the work of a composer. Often, a songwriter will perform his or her own songs as well, whether as a singer, a member of a band, or both. Playing guitar has helped Beth in the writing of lyrics and music. "My songwriting has become more sophisticated as my playing has become more sophisticated," she says.

For most songwriters, writing a song is only the first part of their job. After a song is written, songwriters usually produce a "demo" of the song, so that the client or potential purchaser of the song can hear how it sounds. Songwriters contract with recording studios, studio musicians, and recording engineers to produce a version of the song. The songwriter then submits the song to a publishing house, record company, recording artist, film studio, or others, who will then decide if the song is appropriate for their needs. Often, a songwriter will produce several versions of a song, or submit several different songs for a particular project. There is always a chance that one, some, or all of their songs will be rejected.

Requirements

High School

You should take courses in music that involve you with singing, playing instruments, and studying the history of music. Theater and speech classes will help you to understand the nature of performing, as well as involve you in writing dramatic pieces. You should study poetry in an English class, and try your hand at composing poetry in different forms. Language skills can also be honed in foreign-language classes and by working on student literary magazines. An understanding of how people act and think can influence you as a lyricist, so take courses in psychology and sociology.

Postsecondary Training

There are no real requirements for entering the field of songwriting. All songwriters, however, will benefit from musical training, including musical theory and musical notation. Learning to play one or more instruments, such as the piano or guitar, will be especially helpful in writing songs. Not all songwriters need to be able to sing, but this is helpful.

Songwriting is an extremely competitive field. Despite a lack of formal educational requirements, prospective songwriters are encouraged to continue their education through high school and preferably towards a college degree. Much of the musical training a songwriter needs, however, can also be learned informally. In general, you should have a background in music theory, and in arrangement and orchestration for multiple instruments. You should be able to read music, and be able to write it in the proper musical notation. You should have a good sense of the sounds each type of musical instrument produces, alone and in combination. Understanding harmony is important, as well as a proficiency in or understanding of a variety of styles of music. For example, you should know what makes rock different from reggae, blues, or jazz. Studies in music history will also help develop this understanding.

On the technical side, you should understand the various features, capabilities, and requirements of modern recording techniques. You should be familiar with MIDI and computer technology, as these play important roles in composing, playing, and recording music today.

There are several organizations that help lyricists, songwriters, and composers. The National Academy of Songwriters offers weekly song evaluation workshops in California. The Nashville Songwriters Association offers workshops, seminars, and other services, as well as giving annual awards to songwriters. The Songwriters and Lyricists Club in New York provides contacts for songwriters with music-business professionals. These, and other organizations, offer songwriting workshops and other training seminars.

Other Requirements

Many elements of songwriting cannot really be learned but are a matter of inborn talent. A creative imagination and the ability to invent melodies and combine melodies into a song are essential parts of a songwriting career. As you become more familiar with your own talents, and with songwriting, you'll learn to develop and enhance your creative skills.

"I enjoy observing," Beth says. "I also enjoy the challenge of finding the most succinct way of saying something and making it poetic. I enjoy the process of finding that perfect turn of phrase. I really love language and words."

Exploring

The simplest way to gain experience in songwriting is to learn to play a musical instrument, especially the piano or guitar, and to invent your own songs. Joining a rock group is a way to gain experience writing music for several musicians. Most schools and communities have orchestras, bands, and choruses that are open to performers. Working on a student-written musical show is ideal training for the future songwriter.

If you have your own computer, think about investing in software, a keyboard, and other devices that will allow you to experiment with sounds, recording, and writing and composing your own songs. While much of this equipment is highly expensive, there are plenty of affordable keyboards, drum machines, and software available today. Your school's music department may also have such equipment available.

Employers

Most songwriters work freelance, competing for contracts to write songs for a particular artist, television show, video program, or for contracts with musical publishers and advertising agencies. They will meet with clients to determine the nature of the project and to get an idea of what kind of music the client seeks, the budget for the project, the time in which the project is expected to be completed, and in what form the work is to be submitted. Many songwriters work under contract with one or more music publishing houses. Usually, they must fulfill a certain quota of new songs each year. These songwriters receive a salary, called an advance or draw, that is often paid by the week. Once a song has been published, the money earned by the song goes to pay back the songwriter's draw. A percentage of the money earned by the song over and above the amount of the draw goes to the songwriter as a royalty. Other songwriters are employed by so-called "jingle houses," that is, companies that supply music for advertising commercials. Whereas most songwriters work in their own homes or offices, these songwriters work at the jingle house's offices. Film, television, and video production studios may also employ songwriters on their staff.

Starting Out

Songwriting is a very competitive career and difficult to break into for a beginner. The number of high-paying projects is limited. Often, beginning songwriters start their careers writing music for themselves or as part of a musical group. They may also offer their services to student films, student and local theater productions, church groups, and other religious and non-profit organizations, often for free or for a low fee.

Many songwriters get their start while performing their own music in clubs and other places; they may be approached by a music publisher, who contracts them for a number of songs. Other songwriters record demos of their songs and try to interest record companies and music publishers. Some songwriters organize showcase performances, renting a local club or hall and inviting music industry people to hear their work. Songwriters may have to approach many companies and publishers before they find one willing to buy their songs. A great deal of making a success in songwriting is in developing contacts with people active in the music industry.

Some songwriters get their start in one of the few entry-level positions available. Songwriters aspiring to become composers for film and television can find work as orchestrators or copyists in film houses. Other songwriters may find work for music agents and publishers, which will give them an understanding of the industry and increase their contacts in the industry, as they develop their songwriting skills. Those interested in specializing in advertising jingles may find entry level work as music production assistants with a jingle house. At first, such jobs may involve making coffee, doing paperwork, and completing other clerical tasks. As you gain more exposure to the process of creating music, you may begin in basic areas of music production, or assist experienced songwriters.

Advancement

It is important for a songwriter to develop a strong portfolio of work and a reputation for professionalism. Songwriters who establish a reputation for the quality of their work will receive larger and higher-paying projects as their careers proceed. They may be contracted to score major motion pictures, or to write songs for major recording artists. Ultimately, they may be able to support themselves on their songwriting alone and also have the ability to pick and choose the projects they will work on.

In order to continue to grow with the music industry, songwriters must be tuned into new musical styles and trends. They must also keep up with developments in music technology. A great deal of time is spent making and maintaining contacts with others in the music industry.

Songwriters specializing in jingles and other commercial products may eventually start up their own jingle house. Other songwriters, especially those who have written a number of hit songs, may themselves become recording artists.

For many songwriters, however, success and advancement is a very personal process. A confidence in your own talent will help you to create better work. "I'm not as vulnerable about my work," Beth says. "And I want to open up my subject matter, to expand and experiment more."

Earnings

Songwriters' earnings vary widely, from next to nothing to many millions of dollars. A beginning songwriter may work for free, or for low pay, just to gain experience. A songwriter may sell a jingle to an advertising agency for $1,000 or may receive many thousands of dollars if their work is well-known. Royalties from a song may reach $20,000 per year or more per song, and a successful songwriter may earn $100,000 or more per year from the royalties of several songs. A songwriter's earnings may come from a combination of royalties earned on songs and fees earned from commercial projects.

Those starting as assistants in music production companies or jingle houses may earn as little as $20,000 per year. Experienced songwriters at these companies may earn $50,000 per year or more.

Because most songwriters are freelance, they will have to provide their own health insurance, life insurance, and pension plans. They are usually paid per project, and therefore receive no overtime pay. When facing a deadline, they may have to work many more hours than 8 hours a day or 40 hours a week. Also, songwriters are generally responsible for recording their own demos and must pay for recording studio time, studio musicians, and production expenses.

Work Environment

Songwriters generally possess a strong love for music, and regardless of the level of their success, usually find fulfillment in their careers because they are doing what they love to do. As a freelancer, you'll have control over how you spend your day. You'll work out of your own home or office. You will have your own instruments, and possibly your own recording equipment as well. You may also work in recording studios, where conditions can vary, from noisy and busy, to relaxed and quiet.

Writing music can be stressful. When facing a deadline, you may experience a great deal of pressure while trying to get your music just right and on time. You may face a great deal of rejection before you find someone willing to publish or record your songs. Rejection remains a part of the songwriter's life, even after success.

Many songwriters will work many years with limited or no success. On the other hand, songwriters experience the joys of creativity, which has its own rewards.

Outlook

Most songwriters are unable to support themselves from their songwriting alone and must hold other part-time or full-time jobs while writing songs in their spare time. The competition in this industry is extremely intense, and there are many more songwriters than paying projects. This situation is expected to continue into the next decade.

There are a few bright spots for songwriters. The recent rise of independent filmmaking has created more venues for songwriters to compose film scores. Cable television also provides more opportunities for songwriting, both in the increased number of advertisements and in the growing trend for cable networks to develop their own original programs. Many computer games and software feature songs and music, and this area should grow rapidly in the next decade. Another potential boom area is the World Wide Web. As more and more companies, organizations, and individuals set up multimedia Web sites, there may be an increased demand for songwriters to create songs and music for these sites. Songwriters with MIDI capability will be in the strongest position to benefit from the growth created by computer uses of music. In another field, legalized gambling has spread to many states in the country, a large number of resorts and theme parks have opened, and as these venues produce their own musical theater and shows, they will require more songwriters.

Success in songwriting is a combination of hard work, industry connections, and good luck. The number of hit songs is very small compared to the number of songwriters trying to write them.

For More Information

For information about the professional associations that serve songwriters, contact the following:

American Society of Composers, Authors, and Publishers (ASCAP)
One Lincoln Plaza
New York, NY 10023
Tel: 212-621-6000
Web: http://www.ascap.org

Visit the Songwriter's section of the BMI Web site to learn more about performing rights, music publishing, copyright, and the business of songwriting.

Broadcast Music Inc. (BMI)
320 West 57th Street
New York, NY 10019-3790
Tel: 212-586-2000
Web: http://www.bmi.com

For information about educational seminars, and to read **Musepaper,** *an industry newsletter, visit the academy's Web site, or contact:*

National Academy of Songwriters
6255 Sunset Boulevard, Suite 1023
Hollywood, CA 90028
Tel: 800-826-7287
Email: nassong@aol.com
Web: http://www.nassong.org

To learn about the annual young composer's competition, and other contests, contact:

National Association of Composers USA
PO Box 49256, Barrington Station
Los Angeles, CA 90049
Tel: 310-541-8213
Web: http://www.thebook.com/nacusa/index.html

Technical Writers and Editors

School Subjects
Business
English

Personal Skills
Communication/ideas
Technical/scientific

Work Environment
Primarily indoors
Primarily one location

Minimum Education Level
Bachelor's degree

Salary Range
$28,600 to $44,800 to $72,000

Certification or Licensing
None available

Outlook
Faster than the average

Overview

Technical writers, sometimes called *technical communicators,* express technical and scientific ideas in easy-to-understand language. *Technical editors* revise written text to correct any errors and make it read smoothly and clearly. They also may coordinate the activities of technical writers, technical illustrators, and other staff in preparing material for publication and oversee the document development and production processes.

History

Humans have used writing as a means to communicate information for over 5,500 years. Technical writing, though, did not emerge as a specific profession in the United States until the early years of the 20th century. Before that time, engineers, scientists, and researchers did any necessary writing themselves.

During the early 1900s, technology rapidly expanded. The use of machines to manufacture and mass-produce a wide number of products paved the way for more complex and technical products. Scientists and researchers were discovering new technologies and applications for technology, particularly in electronics, medicine, and engineering. The need to record studies and research, and report them to others, grew. Also, as products became more complex, it was necessary to provide information that documented their components, showed how they were assembled, and explained how to install, use, and repair them. By the mid-1920s, writers were being used to help engineers and scientists document their work and prepare technical information for nontechnical audiences.

Editors had been used for many years to work with printers and authors. They often checked copies of a printed document to correct any errors made during printing, to rewrite unclear passages, and to correct errors in spelling, grammar, and punctuation. As the need for technical writers grew, so too did the need for technical editors. Editors became more involved in documents before the printing stage and worked closely with writers as they prepared their materials. Today, many editors coordinate the activities of all the people involved in preparing technical communications and manage the document development and production processes.

The need for technical writers grew still more with the growth of the computer industry beginning in the 1960s. Originally, many computer companies used computer programmers to write user manuals and other documentation. It was widely assumed that the material was so complex that only those who were involved with creating computer programs would be able to write about them. Although computer programmers had the technical knowledge, many were not able to write clear, easy-to-use manuals. Complaints about the difficulty using and understanding manuals were common. By the 1970s, computer companies began to hire technical writers to write computer manuals and documents. Today, this is one of the largest areas in which technical writers are employed.

The need for technical marketing writers also grew as a result of expanding computer technology. Many copywriters who worked for advertising agencies and marketing firms did not have the technical background to be able to describe the features of the technical products that were coming to market. Thus grew the need for writers who could combine the ability to promote products with the ability to communicate technical information.

The nature of technical writers' and technical editors' jobs continues to change with emerging technologies. Today, the ability to store, transmit, and receive information through computers and electronic means is changing the very nature of documents. Traditional books and paper documents are being replaced by floppy disks, CD-ROMs, interactive multimedia documents, and material accessed through bulletin board systems, faxes, the World Wide Web, and the Internet.

The Job

Technical writers and editors prepare a wide variety of documents and materials. The most common types of documents they produce are manuals, technical reports, specifications, and proposals. Some technical writers also write scripts for videos and audiovisual presentations and text for multimedia programs. Technical writers and editors prepare manuals that give instructions and detailed information on how to install, assemble, use, service, or repair a product or equipment. They may write and edit manuals as simple as a two-page leaflet that gives instructions on how to assemble a bicycle or as complex as a 500-page document that tells service technicians how to repair machinery, medical equipment, or a climate-control system. One of the most common types of manuals is the computer software manual, which informs users on how to load software on their computers, explains how to use the program, and gives information on different features.

Technical writers and editors also prepare technical reports on a multitude of subjects. These reports include documents that give the results of research and laboratory tests and documents that describe the progress of a project. They also write and edit sales proposals, product specifications, quality standards, journal articles, in-house style manuals, and newsletters.

The work of a technical writer begins when he or she is assigned to prepare a document. The writer meets with members of an account or technical team to learn the requirements for the document, the intended purpose or objectives, and the audience. During the planning stage, the writer learns when the document needs to be completed, approximately how long it should be, whether artwork or illustrations are to be included, who the other team members are, and any other production or printing requirements. A schedule is created that defines the different stages of development and determines when the writer needs to have certain parts of the document ready.

The next step in document development is the research, or information gathering, phase. During this stage, technical writers gather all the available information about the product or subject, read and review it, and determine what other information is needed. They may research the topic by reading technical publications, but in most cases they will need to gather information directly from the people working on the product. Writers meet with and interview people who are sources of information, such as scientists, engineers, software developers, computer programmers, managers, and project managers. They ask questions, listen, and take notes or tape record interviews. They gather any available notes, drawings, or diagrams that may be useful.

After writers gather all the necessary information, they sort it out and organize it. They plan how they are going to present the information and prepare an outline for the document. They may decide how the document will look and prepare the design, format, and layout of the pages. In some cases, this may be done by an editor rather than the writer. If illustrations, diagrams, or photographs are going to be included, either the editor or writer makes arrangements for an illustrator, photographer, or art researcher to produce or obtain them.

Then, the writer starts writing and prepares a rough draft of the document. If the document is very large, a writer may prepare it in segments. Once the rough draft is completed, it is submitted to a designated person or group for technical review. Copies of the draft are distributed to managers, engineers, or subject matter experts who can easily determine if any technical information is inaccurate or missing. These reviewers read the document and suggest changes.

The rough draft is also given to technical editors for review of a variety of factors. The editors check that the material is organized well, that each section flows with the section before and after it, and that the language is appropriate for the intended audience. They also check for correct use of grammar, spelling, and punctuation. They ensure that names of parts or objects are consistent throughout the document and that references are accurate. They also check the labeling of graphs and captions for accuracy. Technical editors use special symbols, called proofreader's marks, to indicate the types of changes needed.

The editor and reviewers return their copies of the document to the technical writer. The writer incorporates the appropriate suggestions and revisions and prepares the final draft. The final draft is once again submitted to a designated reviewer or team of reviewers. In some cases, the technical reviewer may do a quick check to make sure that the requested changes were made. In other cases, the technical reviewer may examine the document in depth to ensure technical accuracy and correctness. A walkthrough, or test of the document, may be done for certain types of documents. For example, a walkthrough may be done for a document that explains how to assemble a product. A tester assembles the product by following the instructions given in the document. The tester makes a note of all sections that are unclear or inaccurate, and the document is returned to the writer for any necessary revisions.

For some types of documents, a legal review may also be done. For example, a pharmaceutical company that is preparing a training manual to teach its sales representatives about a newly released drug needs to ensure that all materials are in compliance with Food and Drug Administration (FDA) requirements. A member of the legal department who is familiar with these requirements will review the document to make sure that all information in the document conforms to FDA rules.

Once the final draft has been approved, the document is submitted to the technical editor who makes a comprehensive and detailed check of the document. In addition to checking that the language is clear and reads smoothly, the editor makes sure the table of contents matches the different sections or chapters of a document, all illustrations and diagrams are correctly placed, all captions are matched to the correct picture, consistent terminology is used, and correct references are used in the bibliography and text.

The editor returns the document to either the writer or a word processor who makes any necessary corrections. This copy is then checked by a proofreader. The proofreader compares the final copy against the editor's marked-up copy and makes sure that all changes were made. The document is then prepared for printing. In some cases, the writer is responsible for preparing camera-ready copy or electronic files for printing purposes, and in other cases, a print production coordinator prepares all material to submit to a printer.

Some technical writers specialize in a specific type of material. Technical marketing writers create promotional and marketing materials for technological products. They may write the copy for an advertisement for a technical product, such as a computer workstation or software, or write press releases about the product. They also write sales literature, product flyers, Web pages, and multimedia presentations.

Other technical writers prepare scripts for videotapes and films about technical subjects. These writers, called scriptwriters, need to have an understanding of film and video production techniques.

Some technical writers and editors prepare articles for scientific, medical, computer, or engineering trade journals. These articles may report the results of research conducted by doctors, scientists, or engineers or report on technological advances in a particular field. Some technical writers and editors also develop textbooks. They may receive articles written by engineers or scientists and edit and revise them to make them more suitable for the intended audience.

Technical writers and editors may create documents for a variety of media. Electronic media, such as compact discs and online services, are increasingly being used in place of books and paper documents. Technical writers may create materials that are accessed through bulletin board systems and the Internet or create computer-based resources, such as help menus on computer programs. They also create interactive, multimedia documents that are distributed on compact discs or floppy disks. Some of these media require knowledge of special computer programs that allow material to be hyperlinked, or electronically cross-referenced.

Requirements

High School

In high school, you should take composition, grammar, literature, creative writing, journalism, social studies, math, statistics, engineering, computer science, and as many science classes as possible. Business courses are also useful as they explain the organizational structure of companies and how they operate.

Postsecondary Training

Most employers prefer to hire technical writers and editors who have bachelor's or advanced degrees. Many technical editors graduate with degrees in the humanities, especially English or journalism. Technical writers typically need to have a strong foundation in engineering, computers, or science. Many technical writers graduate with degrees in engineering or science and take classes in technical writing.

Many different types of college programs are available that prepare people to become technical writers and editors. A growing number of colleges are offering degrees in technical writing. Schools without a technical writing program may offer degrees in journalism or English. Programs are offered through English, communications, and journalism departments. Classes vary based on the type of program. In general, classes for technical writers include a core curriculum in writing and classes in algebra, statistics, logic, science, engineering, and computer programming languages. Useful classes for editors include technical writing, project management, grammar, proofreading, copyediting, and print production.

Many technical writers and editors earn master's degrees. In these programs, they study technical writing in depth and may specialize in a certain area, such as scriptwriting, instructional design, or multimedia applications. In addition, many nondegree writing programs are offered to technical writers and editors to hone their skills. Offered as extension courses or continuing education courses, these programs include courses on indexing, editing medical materials, writing for trade journals, and other related subjects.

Technical writers, and occasionally technical editors, are often asked to present samples of their work. College students should build a portfolio during their college years in which they collect their best samples from work that they may have done for a literary magazine, newsletter, or yearbook.

Technical writers and editors should be willing to pursue learning throughout their careers. As technology changes, technical writers and editors may need to take classes to update their knowledge. Changes in electronic printing and computer technology will also change the way technical writers and editors do their jobs and they may need to take courses to learn new skills or new technologies.

Other Requirements

Technical writers need to have good communications skills, science and technical aptitudes, and the ability to think analytically. Technical editors also need to have good communications skills, and judgment, as well as the ability to identify and correct errors in written material. They need to be diplomatic, assertive, and able to explain tactfully what needs to be corrected to writers, engineers, and other people involved with a document. Technical editors should be able to understand technical information easily, but they need less scientific and technical backgrounds than writers. Both technical writers and editors need to be able to work as part of a team and collaborate with others on a project. They need to be highly self-motivated, well organized, and able to work under pressure.

Exploring

If you enjoy writing and are considering a career in technical writing or editing, you should make writing a daily activity. Writing is a skill that develops over time and through practice. Students can keep journals, join writing clubs, and practice different types of writing, such as scriptwriting and informative reports. Sharing writing with others and asking them to critique it is especially helpful. Comments from readers on what they enjoyed about a piece of writing or difficulty they had in understanding certain sections provides valuable feedback that helps to improve your writing style.

Reading a variety of materials is also helpful. Reading exposes you to both good and bad writing styles and techniques and helps you to identify why one approach works better than another.

You may also gain experience by working on a literary magazine, student newspaper, or yearbook (or starting one of your own if one is not available). Both writing and editing articles and managing production give you the opportunity to learn new skills and to see what is involved in preparing documents and other materials.

Students may also be able to get internships, cooperative education assignments, or summer or part-time jobs as proofreaders or editorial assistants that may include writing responsibilities.

Employers

Employment may be found in many different types of places, such as in the fields of aerospace, computers, engineering, pharmacy, and research and development, or with the nuclear industry, medical publishers, government agencies or contractors, and colleges and universities. The aerospace, engineering, medical, and computer industries hire significant numbers of technical writers and editors. So does the federal government, particularly in the departments of Defense and Agriculture, the National Aeronautics and Space Administration (NASA), and the Atomic Energy Commission.

Starting Out

Many technical writers start their careers as scientists, engineers, technicians, or research assistants and move into writing after several years of experience in those positions. Technical writers with a bachelor's degree in a technical subject such as engineering may be able to find work as a technical writer immediately upon graduating from college, but many employers prefer to hire writers with some work experience.

Technical editors who graduate with a bachelor's degree in English or journalism may find entry-level work as editorial assistants, copy editors, or proofreaders. From these positions they are able to move into technical editing positions. Or beginning workers may find jobs as technical editors in small companies or those with a small technical communications department.

If you plan to work for the federal government, you need to pass an examination. Information about examinations and job openings is available at federal employment centers.

You may learn about job openings through your college's job placement services and want ads in newspapers and professional magazines. You may also research companies that hire technical writers and editors and apply directly to them. Many libraries provide useful job resource guides and directories that provide information about companies that hire in specific areas.

Advancement

As technical writers and editors gain experience, they move into more challenging and responsible positions. At first, they may work on simple documents or be assigned to work on sections of a document. As they demonstrate their proficiency and skills, they are given more complex assignments and are responsible for more activities.

Technical writers and editors with several years of experience may move into project management positions. As project managers, they are responsible for the entire document development and production processes. They schedule and budget resources and assign writers, editors, illustrators, and other workers to a project. They monitor the schedule, supervise workers, and ensure that costs remain in budget.

Technical writers and editors who show good project management skills, leadership abilities, and good interpersonal skills may become supervisors or managers. Both technical writers and editors can move into senior writer and senior editor positions. These positions involve increased responsibilities and may include supervising other workers.

Many technical writers and editors seek to develop and perfect their skills rather than move into management or supervisory positions. As they gain a reputation for their quality of work, they may be able to select choice assignments. They may learn new skills as a means of being able to work in new areas. For example, a technical writer may learn a new desktop program in order to become more proficient in designing. Or, a technical writer may learn a hypermedia or hypertext computer program in order to be able to create a multimedia program. Technical writers and editors who broaden their skill base and capabilities can move to higher-paying positions within their own company or at another company. They also may work as free-lancers or set up their own communications companies.

Earnings

In the late 1990s, the average salary for technical writers and editors was $48,000. Salaries for entry-level technical writers and editors ranged from slightly less than $28,600 to more than $44,800. Writers and editors with more than 10 years of experience earned annual salaries between $45,000 and $67,000, with senior writers and editors with management responsibil-ities earning salaries as high as $72,000 a year. The average annual salary for technical writers and editors in the federal government was $47,440 in 1996. Writers and editors in the computer industry earn slightly higher salaries than in other industries. In general, writers and editors who work for firms with large writing staffs earn more than those who work at companies with less than ten writers and editors.

Most companies offer benefits that include paid holidays and vacations, medical insurance, and 401(k) plans. They may also offer profit sharing, pension plans, and tuition assistance programs.

Work Environment

Technical writers and editors usually work in an office environment, with well-lighted and quiet surroundings. They may have their own offices or share work space with other writers and editors. Most writers and editors have computers. They may be able to utilize the services of support staff who can word process revisions, run off copies, fax material, and perform other administrative func-tions or they may have to perform all of these tasks themselves.

Some technical writers and editors work out of home offices and use computer modems and networks to send and receive materials electronical-ly. They may go in to the office only on occasion for meetings and gathering information. Freelancers and contract workers may work at a company's premises or at home.

Although the standard workweek is 40 hours, many technical writers and editors frequently work 50 or 60 hours a week. Job interruptions, meet-ings, and conferences can prevent writers from having long periods of time to write. Therefore, many writers work after hours or bring work home. Both writers and editors frequently work in the evening or on weekends in order to meet a deadline.

In many companies there is pressure to produce documents as quickly as possible. Both technical writers and editors may feel at times that they are compromising the quality of their work due to the need to conform to time and budget constraints. In some companies, technical writers and editors may have increased workloads due to company reorganizations or downsizing. They may need to do the work that was formerly done by more than one person. Technical writers and editors also are increasingly assuming roles and responsibilities formerly performed by other people and this can increase work pressures and stress.

Despite these pressures, most technical writers and editors gain immense satisfaction from their work and the roles that they perform in producing technical communications.

Outlook

The writing and editing field is generally very competitive. Each year, there are more people trying to enter this field than there are available openings. The field of technical writing and editing, though, offers more opportunities than other areas of writing and editing, such as book publishing or journalism. Employment opportunities for technical writers and editors are expected to increase slightly in the coming years. Demand is growing for technical writers who can produce well-written computer manuals. In addition to the computer industry, the pharmaceutical industry is showing an increased need for technical writers. Currently, around 50,000 people are employed as technical writers and editors.

Writers may find positions that include duties in addition to writing. A growing trend is for companies to use writers to run a department, supervise other writers, and manage freelance writers and outside contractors. In addition, many writers are acquiring responsibilities that include desktop publishing and print production coordination.

The demand for technical writers and editors is significantly affected by the economy. During recessionary times, technical writers and editors are often among the first to be let go. Many companies today are continuing to downsize or reduce their number of employees and are reluctant to keep writers on staff. Such companies prefer to hire writers and editors on a temporary contract basis, using them only as long as it takes to complete an assigned document. Technical writers and editors who work on a temporary or freelance basis need to market their services and continually look for new assignments. They also do not have the security or benefits offered by full-time employment.

For More Information

For information on careers, please contact:

Society for Technical Communication
901 North Stuart Street, Suite 904
Arlington, VA 22203
Tel: 703-522-4114
Email: stc@stc-va.org
Web: http://www.stc-va.org

Writers

English Journalism	School Subjects
Communication/ideas Helping/teaching	Personal Skills
Primarily indoors Primarily one location	Work Environment
Bachelor's degree	Minimum Education Level
$21,000 to $30,000 to $75,000+	Salary Range
None available	Certification or Licensing
Faster than the average	Outlook

Overview

Writers are involved with expressing, editing, promoting, and interpreting ideas and facts in written form for books, magazines, trade journals, newspapers, technical studies and reports, company newsletters, radio and television broadcasts, and advertisements.

Writers develop fiction and nonfiction ideas for plays, novels, poems, and other related works; report, analyze, and interpret facts, events, and personalities; review art, music, drama, and other artistic presentations; and persuade the general public to choose or favor certain goods, services, and personalities.

History

The skill of writing has existed for thousands of years. Papyrus fragments with writing by ancient Egyptians date from about 3000 BC, and archaeological findings show that the Chinese had developed books by about 1300

BC. A number of technical obstacles had to be overcome before printing and the profession of writing evolved. Books of the Middle Ages were copied by hand on parchment. The ornate style that marked these books helped ensure their rarity. Also, few people were able to read. Religious fervor prohibited the reproduction of secular literature.

The development of the printing press by Johannes Gutenberg (1400?-1468?) in the middle of the 15th century and the liberalism of the Protestant Reformation, which helped encourage a wider range of publications, greater literacy, and the creation of a number of works of literary merit, helped develop the publishing industry. The first authors worked directly with printers.

The modern publishing age began in the 18th century. Printing became mechanized, and the novel, magazine, and newspaper developed. The first newspaper in the American colonies appeared in the early 18th century, but it was Benjamin Franklin (1706-1790) who, as editor and writer, made the *Pennsylvania Gazette* one of the most influential in setting a high standard for his fellow American journalists. Franklin also published the first magazine in the colonies, *The American Magazine,* in 1741.

Advances in the printing trades, photoengraving, retailing, and the availability of capital produced a boom in newspapers and magazines in the 19th century. Further mechanization in the printing field, such as the use of the Linotype machine, high-speed rotary presses, and special color reproduction processes, set the stage for still further growth in the book, newspaper, and magazine industry.

In addition to the print media, the broadcasting industry has contributed to the development of the professional writer. Film, radio and television are sources of entertainment, information, and education that provide employment for thousands of writers.

The Job

Writers work in the field of communications. Specifically, they deal with the written word, whether it is destined for the printed page, broadcast, computer screen, or live theater. The nature of their work is as varied as the materials they produce: books, magazines, trade journals, newspapers, technical reports, company newsletters and other publications, advertisements, speeches, scripts for motion picture and stage productions, and scripts for radio and television broadcast. Writers develop ideas and write for all media.

Prose writers for newspapers, magazines, and books share many of the same duties. First they come up with an idea for an article or book from their own interests or are assigned a topic by an editor. The topic is of relevance to the particular publication; for example, a writer for a magazine on parenting may be assigned an article on car seat safety. Then writers begin gathering as much information as possible about the subject through library research, interviews, the Internet, observation, and other methods. They keep extensive notes from which they will draw material for their project. Once the material has been organized and arranged in logical sequence, writers prepare a written outline. The process of developing a piece of writing is exciting, although it can also involve detailed and solitary work. After researching an idea, a writer might discover that a different perspective or related topic would be more effective, entertaining, or marketable.

When working on assignment, writers submit their outlines to an editor or other company representative for approval. Then they write a first draft of the manuscript, trying to put the material into words that will have the desired effect on their audience. They often rewrite or polish sections of the material as they proceed, always searching for just the right way of imparting information or expressing an idea or opinion. A manuscript may be reviewed, corrected, and revised numerous times before a final copy is submitted. Even after that, an editor may request additional changes.

Writers for newspapers, magazines, or books often specialize in their subject matter. Some writers might have an educational background that allows them to give critical interpretations or analyses. For example, a health or science writer for a newspaper typically has a degree in biology and can interpret new ideas in the field for the average reader.

Columnists/commentators analyze news and social issues. They write about events from the standpoint of their own experience or opinion. *Critics* review literary, musical, or artistic works and performances. *Editorial writers* write on topics of public interest, and their comments, consistent with the viewpoints and policies of their employers, are intended to stimulate or mold public opinion. *Newswriters* work for newspapers, radio, or TV news departments, writing news stories from notes supplied by reporters or wire services.

Corporate writers and writers for nonprofit organizations have a wide variety of responsibilities. These writers may work in such places as a large insurance corporation or for a small nonprofit religious group where they may be required to write news releases, annual reports, speeches for the company head, or public relations materials. Typically they are assigned a topic with length requirements for a given project. They may receive raw research materials, such as statistics, and are expected to conduct additional research, including personal interviews. These writers must be able to write quickly and accurately on short deadlines, while also working with people whose primary job is not in the communications field. The written work is submitted to a supervisor and often a legal department for approval; rewrites are a normal part of this job.

Copywriters write copy that is primarily designed to sell goods and services. Their work appears as advertisements in newspapers, magazines, and other publications or as commercials on radio and television broadcasts. Sales and marketing representatives first provide information on the product and help determine the style and length of the copy. The copywriters conduct additional research and interviews; to formulate an effective approach, they study advertising trends and review surveys of consumer preferences. Armed with this information, copywriters write a draft that is submitted to the account executive and the client for approval. The copy is often returned for correction and revision until everyone involved is satisfied. Copywriters, like corporate writers, may also write articles, bulletins, news releases, sales letters, speeches, and other related informative and promotional material. Many copywriters are employed in advertising agencies. They also may work for public relations firms or in communications departments of large companies.

Technical writers can be divided into two main groups: those who convert technical information into material for the general public, and those who convey technical information between professionals. Technical writers in the first group may prepare service manuals or handbooks, instruction or repair booklets, or sales literature or brochures; those in the second group may write grant proposals, research reports, contract specifications, or research abstracts.

Screenwriters prepare scripts for motion pictures or television. They select or are assigned a subject, conduct research, write and submit a plot outline and narrative synopsis (treatment), and confer with the producer and/or director about possible revisions. Screenwriters may adapt books or plays for film and television dramatizations. They often collaborate with other screenwriters and may specialize in a particular type of script or writing.

Playwrights do similar writing for the stage. They write dialogue and describe action for plays that may be tragedies, comedies, or dramas, with themes sometimes adapted from fictional, historical, or narrative sources. Playwrights combine the elements of action, conflict, purpose, and resolution to depict events from real or imaginary life. They often make revisions even while the play is in rehearsal.

Continuity writers prepare the material read by radio and television announcers to introduce or connect various parts of their programs.

Novelists and *short story writers* create stories that may be published in books, magazines, or literary journals. They take incidents from their own lives, from news events, or from their imaginations and create characters, settings, actions, and resolutions. *Poets* create narrative, dramatic, or lyric poetry for books, magazines, or other publications, as well as for special events such as commemorations. These writers may work with literary agents or editors who help guide them through the writing process, which includes research of the subject matter and an understanding of the intended audience. Many universities and colleges offer graduate degrees in creative writing. In these programs, students work intensively with published writers to learn the art of storytelling.

Writers can be employed either as in-house staff or as freelancers. Pay varies according to experience and the position, but freelancers must provide their own office space and equipment such as computers and fax machines. Freelancers also are responsible for keeping tax records, sending out invoices, negotiating contracts, and providing their own health insurance.

Requirements

High School

High school courses that are helpful include English, literature, foreign languages, general science, social studies, computer science, and typing. The ability to type is almost a requisite for all positions in the communications field as is familiarity with computers.

Postsecondary Training

Competition for writing jobs almost always demands the background of a college education. Many employers prefer you have a broad liberal arts background or majors in English, literature, history, philosophy, or one of the social sciences. Other employers desire communications or journalism training in college. Occasionally a master's degree in a specialized writing field may be required. A number of schools offer courses in journalism, and some of them offer courses or majors in book publishing, publication management, and newspaper and magazine writing.

In addition to formal course work, most employers look for practical writing experience. If you have served on high school or college newspapers, yearbooks, or literary magazines, you will make a better candidate, as well as if you have worked for small community newspapers or radio stations, even in an unpaid position. Many book publishers, magazines, newspapers, and radio and television stations have summer internship programs that provide valuable training if you want to learn about the publishing and broadcasting businesses. Interns do many simple tasks, such as running errands and answering phones, but some may be asked to perform research, conduct interviews, or even write some minor pieces.

Writers who specialize in technical fields may need degrees, concentrated course work, or experience in specific subject areas. This applies frequently to engineering, business, or one of the sciences. Also, technical communications is a degree now offered at many universities and colleges.

If you wish to enter positions with the federal government, you will have to take a civil service examination and meet certain specified requirements, according to the type and level of position.

Other Requirements

Writers should be creative and able to express ideas clearly, have a broad general knowledge, be skilled in research techniques, and be computer literate. Other assets include curiosity, persistence, initiative, resourcefulness, and an accurate memory. For some jobs—on a newspaper, for example, where the activity is hectic and deadlines short—the ability to concentrate and produce under pressure is essential.

Exploring

As a high school or college student, you can test your interest and aptitude in the field of writing by serving as a reporter or writer on school newspapers, yearbooks, and literary magazines. Various writing courses and workshops offer the opportunity to sharpen writing skills.

Small community newspapers and local radio stations often welcome contributions from outside sources, although they may not have the resources to pay for them. Jobs in bookstores, magazine shops, and even newsstands offer a chance to become familiar with the various publications.

Information on writing as a career may also be obtained by visiting local newspapers, publishers, or radio and television stations and interviewing some of the writers who work there. Career conferences and other guidance programs frequently include speakers on the entire field of communications from local or national organizations.

Employers

Nearly a third of salaried writers and editors work for newspapers, magazines, and book publishers, according to the *Occupational Outlook Handbook*. Writers are also employed by advertising agencies, in radio and television broadcasting, public relations firms, and on journals and newsletters published by business and nonprofit organizations, such as professional associations, labor unions, and religious organizations. Other employers are government agencies and film production companies.

Starting Out

A fair amount of experience is required to gain a high-level position in the field. Most writers start out in entry-level positions. These jobs may be listed with college placement offices, or they may be obtained by applying directly to the employment departments of the individual publishers or broadcasting companies. Graduates who previously served internships with these companies often have the advantage of knowing someone who can give them a personal recommendation. Want ads in newspapers and trade journals are another source for jobs. Because of the competition for positions, however, few vacancies are listed with public or private employment agencies.

Employers in the communications field usually are interested in samples of published writing. These are often assembled in an organized portfolio or scrapbook. Bylined or signed articles are more impressive than stories whose source is not identified.

Beginning positions as a junior writer usually involve library research, preparation of rough drafts for part or all of a report, cataloging, and other related writing tasks. These are generally carried on under the supervision of a senior writer.

Some technical writers have entered the field after working in public relations departments or as technicians or research assistants, then transferring to technical writing as openings occur. Many firms now hire writers directly upon application or recommendation of college professors and placement offices.

Advancement

Most writers find their first jobs as editorial or production assistants. Advancement may be more rapid in small companies, where beginners learn by doing a little bit of everything and may be given writing tasks immediately. In large firms, duties are usually more compartmentalized. Assistants in entry-level positions are assigned such tasks as research, fact checking, and copyrighting, but it generally takes much longer to advance to full-scale writing duties.

Promotion into more responsible positions may come with the assignment of more important articles and stories to write, or it may be the result of moving to another company. Mobility among employees in this field is common. An assistant in one publishing house may switch to an executive position in another. Or a writer may switch to a related field as a type of advancement: from publishing, for example, to teaching, public relations, advertising, radio, or television.

A technical writer can be promoted to positions of responsibility by moving from such jobs as writer to technical editor to project leader or documentation manager. Opportunities in specialized positions also are possible.

Freelance or self-employed writers earn advancement in the form of larger fees as they gain exposure and establish their reputations.

Earnings

In 1996, beginning writers and researchers received starting salaries of about $21,000 a year, according to the Dow Jones Newspaper Fund. Experienced writers and researchers are paid $30,000 and over, depending on their qualifications and the size of the publication they work on. In book publishing, some divisions pay better than others.

The salaries of technical writers are slightly higher than those of other professional writers. In general, the median beginning wage for those with a college degree is $28,600 per year. The salaries of experienced writers ranges from about $45,000 to over $67,000 per year. Earnings of those in administrative and supervisory positions are somewhat higher.

Technical writers working for the federal government average $47,400; other types of writers earn an average of $39,000 a year.

In addition to their salaries, many writers earn some income from freelance work. Part-time freelancers may earn from $5,000 to $15,000 a year. Freelance earnings vary widely. Full-time established freelance writers may earn up to $75,000 a year.

Work Environment

Working conditions vary for writers. Although the workweek usually runs 35 to 40 hours, many writers work overtime. A publication that is issued frequently has more deadlines closer together, creating greater pressures to meet them. The work is especially hectic on newspapers and at broadcasting companies, which operate seven days a week. Writers often work nights and weekends to meet deadlines or to cover a late-developing story.

Most writers work independently, but they often must cooperate with artists, photographers, rewriters, and advertising people who may have widely differing ideas of how the materials should be prepared and presented.

Physical surroundings range from comfortable private offices to noisy, crowded newsrooms filled with other workers typing and talking on the telephone. Some writers must confine their research to the library or telephone interviews, but others may travel to other cities or countries or to local sites, such as theaters, ballparks, airports, factories, or other offices.

The work is arduous, but writers are seldom bored. Each day brings new and interesting problems. The jobs occasionally require travel. The most difficult element is the continual pressure of deadlines. People who are the most content as writers enjoy and work well with deadline pressure.

Outlook

The employment of writers is expected to increase faster than the average rate of all occupations through 2006. The demand for writers by newspapers, periodicals, book publishers, and nonprofit organizations is expected to increase. Advertising and public relations will also provide job opportunities.

The major book and magazine publishers, broadcasting companies, advertising agencies, public relations firms, and the federal government account for the concentration of writers in large cities such as New York, Chicago, Los Angeles, Boston, Philadelphia, San Francisco, and Washington, DC. Opportunities in small newspapers, corporations, and professional, religious, business, technical, and trade publications can be found throughout the country.

People entering this field should realize that the competition for jobs is extremely keen. Beginners, especially, may have difficulty finding employment. Of the thousands who graduate each year with degrees in English, journalism, communications, and the liberal arts, intending to establish a career as writer, many turn to other occupations when they find that applicants far outnumber the job openings available. College students would do well to keep this in mind and prepare for an unrelated alternate career in the event they are unable to obtain a position as writer; another benefit of this approach is that, at the same time, they will become qualified as writers in a specialized field. The practicality of preparing for alternate careers is borne out by the fact that opportunities are best in firms that prepare business and trade publications and in technical writing.

Potential writers who end up working in a different field may be able to earn some income as freelancers, selling articles, stories, books, and possibly TV and movie scripts, but it is usually difficult for anyone to be self-supporting entirely on independent writing.

For More Information

Information on writing and editing careers in the field of science communications is available from:

National Association of Science Writers
PO Box 294
Greenlawn, NY 11740
Tel: 516-757-5664

This organization offers student memberships for those interested in opinion writing.

National Conference of Editorial Writers
6223 Executive Boulevard
Rockville, MD 20852
Tel: 301-984-3015
Web: http://www.ncew.org

Index